LOST
But Not
FOREVER

A Woman Agonizes
for the
Return of Her Husband

Gary Bell
with Davin Read Seay

HARVEST HOUSE PUBLISHERS
Eugene, Oregon 97402

LOST, BUT NOT FOREVER

Copyright ©1981 by Harvest House Publishers
Eugene, Oregon 97402

Library of Congress Catalog Card Number 80-81472
ISBN 0-89081-253-5

Printed in the United States of America.

CONTENTS

CHAPTER ONE

Always the Best

My name is Gary Bell, and the book you're holding is my story. It's my life, but maybe it sounds a little like your life too, since each of us has been touched by tragedy and failure. Maybe you're a victim or maybe you've victimized others, but I'm not going to dwell on the misery. Instead, I'm here to tell you of triumph and victory. In fact, the reason I'm alive today is because of that victory.

As any playwright or dramatist will tell you, there's a fine line between triumph and tragedy, often existing only in the mind of the beholder. Individuals judge for themselves the measure of any person's life. You may read this story and see only the wasted years, the ruined potentials, the damage and destruction. Or you may look beyond to the victory I claim. The choice is yours.

My story is one of extremes. On one side is the Gary Bell of today—a husband, father, and prosperous businessman. I look older than my forty-odd years, my hair is gray, and lines of age are beginning to cross my face. But I'm fit and trim and in the best of health. People who know me say my eyes tell a story of their own.

On the other side of this coin, behind the successful businessman, is a picture of horror and loathing—a living corpse, an old and sick man whose name was also Gary Bell. He shambled along a city street in filthy, ragged clothes. His emaciated, trembling form looked like a concentration-camp victim. Self-abused and dying by degrees, he was lost to everything but the pain he tried to obliterate through self-destruction. You've seen that old man a hundred times yourself, huddled in an alley, clutching his bottle in a paper bag as though it were life itself, mumbling oaths, or talking to his own hallucinations. Perhaps in your compassion and pity you wondered how such a creature could be called human. He was devoid of self-respect, rotting away from the inside, and blind to his own miserable condition. That was the Gary Bell I used to be.

I was born in Chicago as an only child. From outward appearances I had what is generally termed a normal childhood. My family was well-to-do, upper-middle-class, and I had the benefit of most of what money could buy. There was little lacking materially in my life. Yet I sometimes see, when I look back on those early, half-remembered times, intimations of what was to come. It was nothing definite—no single incident I can point to and say, "Yes, that's it; that's where it began." It was only a feeling, a sense of lost innocence, of childhood's joys giving way to ambition sprung up before its time.

I don't pretend to grasp the finer points of human psychology, nor do I particularly enjoy analyzing my past to see what made me tick. I only know that as a boy I excelled at anything I put my hand to. I was resourceful and self-confident to a fault.

Maybe that sounds strange. How can resourcefulness and confidence be counted as faults, especially in a young man? Certainly in the society I grew up in, these qualities made the crucial difference between success and failure. To be a self-starter and to want the best of everything were admirable goals for anyone beginning his life's journey.

Perhaps this kind of desperate self-reliance blinds us to the real needs in our lives, those empty spaces that we can't fill despite our best efforts. I'm no philosopher; I can only look at the fruits of my life and wonder if these seeds provided early clues.

I *was* the best in almost everything—the best in football, basketball, and baseball. Even more importantly, I was first on the playground, the toughest kid in school, and always fighting to keep it that way. Most young boys are naturally aggressive, I suppose, and many of them have a chip on their shoulder. But it was different with me—I *had* to be in control. It was first or nothing at all. I loved the feeling of being king of the mountain, whatever the mountain was. If there was a challenge, I welcomed it. No one forced me to take the leader's role, no one set those standards—not my parents, not the teachers, not the other students. Only my own desire to be and do something special made me want to be first.

Of course, no one can win all the time, and those times that I lost, whether it was by finishing second or tenth place, were unendurably agonizing. I didn't have to face a wrathful father or hear the derisive shouts of my classmates. It was only a voice inside telling me I had lost the game as I myself had defined the rules. There could be no more bitter disappointment, nothing more degrading or demoralizing. For most people, failure is difficult to come to terms with. For me, it was a small death each time it happened.

But it wasn't often that I had to face the specter of my own limitations. In those areas in which I was not naturally gifted I would psyche myself into a winning attitude. As any athlete will tell you, the right attitude is critical to winning; it's as important as concentration, training, and skill. It's not for me to say that the desire to win isn't a good thing. But by the same token no man is complete in himself. In my business, that of finding jobs for qualified executives, I see such men and women every day, and I'm happy to help them realize their goals and ambitions. I would never say to them, "No matter how confident you are in your own abilities, no matter how far you've come or how far you'll go, there will be a time when you need the love and protection of Someone greater than you." What those people believe, and what you believe, is not my business.

Yet if someone had said that to me as a proud and strong young man, fearful of nothing but the idea of failure, I would have laughed loud and long.

Even if it were true.

CHAPTER TWO

Beautiful Tucson

High school turned to college, and college passed swiftly into young adulthood. My school days were marked by football, lazy romances, and a lackluster interest in higher education. It wasn't that I was a poor student, but just that I was more interested in playing tight end and quarterback on school teams. I was a football hero, and that suited me fine—I had lots of buddies, girlfriends, and good times. Like most people, I look back on my school days as happy and carefree, and perhaps a little unreal.

After graduating with a degree in business, I started looking around for a niche to fill my time and energies. I would have liked to go into something that suited my own self-image—a natural-born winner—but before the world could beat a path to my door, I heard a knock from Uncle Sam. The Army didn't appeal to me, so in order to avoid marching my way through military service, I entered the Air Force. But far from soaring around in the wild blue yonder, my stint involved working in a personnel office—not what you might call a challenging occupation.

There was, however, one real benefit that I gained from my time in the Air Force. Shortly after my tour of duty began, my father was transferred by his firm to a new position in Tucson, Arizona. While on leave I went to see my parents, and as soon as I stepped off the plane I knew I had found paradise. If you're from Chicago or some other big city, you understand how it affected me. I landed in a little place called Paradise Valley, and as the doors opened, the sight of that clear blue sky shimmering in the warm air awakened something in me that had long been dormant.

It was *freedom*—a sense of limitless expanses, a lingering feel of the Old West, unhindered and unconfined. It was a range of mountains rising russet, amber, and gold in the distance. It was the aroma of orange blossoms, a scent as delicate and intoxicating as the finest perfume. It was the clean and vibrant air coupled with a vast and unfettered horizon. There may be more beautiful places on this earth, but on that day as I stepped out of the plane, with my duffel bag over my shoulder, you could never have convinced me; I had fallen in love with the Southwest. It was like arriving at last to a home I had never known.

During that first stay in Tucson, my mother and I spent days exploring the natural wonders of the place—the rich history lingering in the ghost towns and old mining outposts; the Indian reservations that spoke of an ancient life; and the desert, awesome in its timeless solitude, with sandstone monuments and cactus armies.

Through a little military horse-trading I got a transfer to Phoenix. I lived on the base there, soaking up the natural splendor, having a good time with my buddies, sliding through my duties, and generally feeling my youthful oats. Yet even in these happy days there were clues of what was to come, suggestions planted like seeds, sprouting and taking shape in the darkness.

I had had the usual run-ins with drinking during my student days—beer busts and all-night parties celebrated on the simplest pretext. I had had my share of queasy stomachs, splitting headaches, and morning-after remorse, and the pattern continued during my time in the Air Force. I didn't notice it then, but now those early-warning signs are painfully clear. I did't get drunk like my buddies did, or for the same reasons. I never liked the taste of alcohol, and I found no pleasure in drinking except for that one important effect: getting drunk. But even that was different: it took a lot more liquor to get me there than it did my friends, and once I arrived I was reluctant to leave.

Maybe I should have known better; maybe I should have been able to make out the writing on the wall, faint as it was. But even if I *had* known what was looming up before me, would I have been able to change my course? Would I have wanted to? I was a firm believer in my own destiny; I was the master of my fate, the captain of my soul. Even if I had recognized forces in this world that could lay me as low as any human being can sink, would I have turned aside?

During the last of my years in the service I met and started going out with an attractive girl named Darlene. As the truism has it, we were in love with the idea of love. Maybe we truly did love each other; I can't really say. People grow wiser as a natural result of getting older, and part of that process is understanding the caring and commitment that are part of true love. Young love is a beautiful thing, but it is full of joy and terror and has a peculiar kind of grace all its own. It may only hint at the selflessness for true giving love. But it is still a wonderful moment in anyone's life as it lights the future with a rosy glow.

Of course, along with the joy of discovery, passion also breeds life's costlier mistakes. So it was with Darlene and me. Physical attractions proved stronger than mutual discretion and I soon found myself marrying Darlene for reasons that had as much to do with saving her from disgrace and salvaging my conscience than with any true love we felt for each other.

But then came the matter of providing for my impending family. I had an honorable discharge and a college education, and I was young, forthright, and energetic. But still there was a problem. In those days Tucson was pretty much a one-horse town, and the name of that horse was Hughes Aircraft. It was not only the largest industry in the area, but it was the *only* one. Everything else was strictly mom-and-pop operations. Darlene, in fact, worked at Hughes and knew firsthand the scarcity of jobs in the on-again, off-again aerospace industry.

In spite of all this, there was no way I was going to leave Tucson. I loved the place too much, and Darlene already had a well-paying job. I was going to make my future there despite the odds against me.

CHAPTER THREE

Into the Force

A couple of fruitless weeks passed while I lived in an old house in downtown Tucson with some friends and prowled the streets looking for work. It was a typically brilliant Arizona morning when I happened across a poster announcing my future in bold type. TUCSON NEEDS QUALIFIED POLICE AND FIREMAN. APPLY TODAY. A few hours later I walked out of police headquarters with a passing grade on the preliminary police examination and an appointment for further tests in my pocket.

You might wonder why I was excited over the prospect of police work. With a business degree and my clerking time in the Air Force, I seemed to have been cut out for a quieter career. But actually I was yearning for adventure, for some excitement in my life, for a ways to prove myself in the world of men. *Action*—it was a magic word, and I was eager to take up the challenge. It came sooner than I expected.

Civil service exams and personality and psychological tests proved to be no barrier. With the doctors I was easily able to anticipate what kind of character makeup they were looking for, just by using a little common sense and acting skill. They weren't after a gung-ho, TV-type cop; loners and "hot dogs" don't work well in the kind of team effort that law enforcement requires. They were looking for idealism, a willingness to serve, and a quick mind. Equally important was a sense of self-confidence, a bold demeanor—a guy who could take care of himself. The psychologists were easy enough to get by, but the veteran cops were another matter.

As with many other occupations, the police force requires an oral exam. The difference between conventional oral exams and those administered by the police is the difference between polite conversation and third-degree grilling. It has to be, of course. Police work, more than almost any other job, requires men who can function well under stress. Verbal intimidation is a common form of stress for a cop.

I had heard rumors that several recruits in my class hadn't gotten past the oral board, and that presented an almost-irresistible challenge to me. Tucson boasts a highly educated police force, and the guys who didn't make it hadn't failed for lack of brains.

I had to use logic. What, I thought to myself, would they be trying to learn about me? It certainly wasn't going to be how well I spoke English. I would have to analyze them carefully, roll with the punches, and stay in control of myself every moment.

I sat in a small room for over an hour under a lamp as hot and glaring as any you've seen in the movies, while a captain and two lieutenants roasted me slowly on a spit of verbal abuse. They prodded mercilessly, prying into my private life, making innuendos and crude suggestions that no one with a speck of pride would sit still for. My childhood, my heritage, personal details of my past, my sexual preferences, my *mother's* sexual preferences—nothing escaped their withering tongues. In language that would put a blush in a truck driver's cheeks, the trio spared me nothing, never letting up, pushing me further and further while all the while I played off them as best I could, turning around their assaults, speaking softly and calmly. It was nerve-wracking exercise in just keeping control. These guys were seasoned pros with a lot of experience, and they had taken to their task with a vengeance.

By remaining as calm as I did, I knew I was playing a tricky game and one that could easily backfire on me. Obviously I couldn't just sit there all afternoon and let them insult my mother; I would lose the job as surely as if I'd blown my top at the first snide remark. They weren't looking for a passive Milquetoast, content to let others more aggressive walk all over his face. I would, if I passed, ultimately represent the City of Tucson to the average citizen on the street, and no authority charged with maintaining order takes abuse indefinitely; respect is an obvious and essential ingredient for law officers.

Somewhere between these two extremes lay the magic combination of traits—tolerant, but not to a fault; levelheaded, but capable of swinging into action. When I finally told them where to get off, it was in no uncertain terms; I didn't stammer, and my face didn't turn red, but I simply let them know I'd had enough in language they could understand. By reaching my boiling point without spilling over into a fistfight or frustrated tears, I had beaten them at their own game. I can still remember the look on their faces when I finally answered their taunts, turning the tables on them, if only briefly. "You gave it your best lick, gentlemen," I thought, "and I'm still around."

The captain leaned over, smiled, and shook my hand. "Well," he said, "looks like you're one of us, Bell. Congratulations. You're going to be a police officer, and a good one at that."

It was over—the humiliating ordeal was finished, and I had emerged a winner. As I walked out into the dry desert afternoon, my shirt was soaked with sweat and I was trembling, but the grin on my face wouldn't go away. Never had the manifest destiny of Gary Bell seemed more sure. I had made it, but I sure felt sorry for any crook trying to keep secrets from those three guys!

After six weeks of intensive training at the police academy, covering everything from Arizona law to marksmanship, I became a patrolman and was assigned a beat in suburban Tucson. At that time Tucson had a large population of sick and dying people. It was ironic that a place of such health and vibrancy should be the home of so many terminal cases, but of course that's exactly why they came there. It was an elixier, that bit of Arizona sun. Many kinds of respiratory disorders called for relocating in the Southwest, to breathe the good air and dry out the clogged passages.

From my vantage point, as a rookie cop, the cure failed just about as often as it succeeded. The resulting high suicide rate was only one of the factors that made up the seamy side of police work for me. Seeing people in every grotesque position of self-inflicted death, shotguns still lodged in their mouths, blood and brains splattered behind them on the walls and furniture, offered me a sobering realization of mortality. Sifting through the victim's personal belongings, with all the debris that clung to them from life, made me feel like an intruder. Asking endless questions of the families, numbed by shock and grief, made me realize that doing my job was often at the expense of other people's feelings and my own sense of decency.

I think of myself as a man who likes people. I get along well with most people, and I really take a delight in being with people. Police work gave me a sense of aversion, almost a repulsion for some of the people I had to deal with. This didn't apply only to the countless drunks, filthy and belligerent, that I had to trundle into the back seat of the squad car for a trip downtown. It didn't apply only to the pimps and petty thieves whom I found myself reluctantly involved with. Any cop will tell you that if he spends enough time on the street, a little of the street will rub off on him. To catch criminals it's often necessary to think like one, and sometimes you just can't turn it off right away.

But it wasn't always the bad guys who turned my stomach, who made me feel like the whole world was just big fish eating little fish, and no one with right on their side. More often than not, the guy who had been burgled or the lady who had been raped or assaulted seemed to have invited his or her bad luck just by being alive. "How could they allow these things to happen to them?" I found myself thinking. Their plight was reflected in their sad eyes—always the same shattered look. They had been victimized by themselves, it seemed to me—by their own hopeless existence, their stupidity, their greed and fear. The victims brought the crimes on themselves, or at least that's how it looked to me as I surveyed their shabby lives, the sordid affairs they became entangled in, and inevitable result—the knife wound, the bullet hole, the bleary face of a weeping woman.

It was a cynicism I quickly adjusted to as part of my job. I tried to keep it from infecting my other relationships or how I acted toward these unfortunate people. I still remember the feeling of revulsion, the urge to shake them and shout into their faces. "What's the matter with you? Pick yourself up! Straighten yourself out before you end up on a slab!" But all the time I would calmly be making out my report, acting concerned and sympathetic.

As you may have guessed, police work was not all it was cracked up to be. As that first year wore on I found myself becoming more and more dissatisfied with the job. It was exciting, to be sure; I can still vividly picture my first high-speed car chase—careening through the streets of Tucson, the siren so loud in my ears I could hardly think, shouting our position into the radio. But we weren't chasing bank robbers or international jewel thieves—just a kid showing off to his girlfriend. Life, even for a cop, can take on a routine, and it was this routine, along with dying and derelict specimens that made up my clientele, that eventually soured my law-enforcement career.

There was, however, one person I met for whom I had a lot of respect—a person who would eventually lead me to life on the other side of the badge.

Aside from being a town for the sick and old, Tucson was also a desert nest for the Mob. Mob operations were not especially extensive in Arizona back then. Most of the heavy action in organized crime took place to the northwest in Las Vegas. But Tucson was a haven for many prominent mobsters who ran their territories and raised their families far from the iniquity they helped to spawn. The homes of these capos were located in some of the swankier sections of suburban Tucson. Yet for all their ostentation—cars, clothes, private schools, and horseback lessons for their kids—they kept a low profile within the community at large.

The Tucson police force, as a matter of policy, kept a running check on some of the more important mobsters located within their jurisdiction. They ran routine surveillances and kept up a low-keyed harassment campaign if for no other reason than to let the bosses know that the police were keeping an eye on things.

As a patrolman on the beat, I was given a list of license-plate numbers to the cars of mobsters and their families. Most of the time they weren't too hard to spot anyway. They were huge, silent limos with dark, one-way glass blocking out the blue and gold of the Arizona day, sliding slowly down quiet neighborhood streets.

Many of the cars I trailed belonged to the prominent East Coast racketeers—kingpins in New Jersey, Brooklyn, and Chicago. I got so that I knew their names and territories pretty well, learning as much as I could about their positions in the various hierarchies of each organization. I enjoyed pulling them over and tying them up over some minor infraction. Most of them were used to it and were skilled at putting up a pleasant, law-abiding facade, even joking about it between themselves or with their chauffeurs.

But when Joey made his offer, I knew he wasn't joking. I knew who he was as soon as I saw the plate numbers—Joey, the son of one of the biggest mob figures of a large, East Coast territory. Young (about my age) and aggressive, he had taken charge of his father's expanding operations in Las Vegas.

Within the tightly knit business family, where nepotism was the order of the day, Joey was the heir-apparent.

Gravel crunched under my shoes and a brilliant Southwestern sun threw down shimmering heat waves on the limo's shiny surface as I walked over slowly to the long car and asked to see the chauffeur's license.

"There's a problem, officer?" a voice said from the darkened back seat.

"Just routine," I answered, leaning down and trying to make out his face. The back door opened next to me, and he stepped out into the heat and glare.

"Something I can help you with?" he said, and introduced himself.

For a long moment we appraised each other as a dry wind whipped along the road. I had pulled him over just outside of town, close to the state highway, and periodically large trucks would come ripping past, bringing in their wake of flurry of dust and pebbles.

We were remarkably the same, he and I. We were not only the same age, but had a similar physique and the same easygoing, self-assured manner. He stood by the side of the road, looking me up and down, with a long, measured stare, and I suppose I did pretty much the same.

"So you're Joey," I thought to myself and nodded in silent approval. His tailored suit fit him with an easy luxury. His dark hair and eyes glistened in the bright light, and I could smell the odor of expensive cologne. From the car came the rich scent of leather upholstery and aged cigars. He exuded an aura of power—dangerous power handled easily and cannily. He was accustomed to the circles he traveled in, making decisions involving millions of dollars, death and life, killing and sparing.

Next to him, my symbols of authority—my badge and service revolver, my uniform—seemed trivial and helpless. I had no doubt that Joey did his job with casual ease, perhaps even wearing the same winning smile. The idea in no way upset me; I was immediately fascinated with this mirror image, if you will, staring back at me from the other side of real success. That, I thought to myself, is where I should be—wearing those clothes, being driven in that car, making those decisons. I never gave a thought to the source of Joey's wealth—the generations of human exploitation, greed, and brutality that had gone into putting him and others like him where they were. For the moment that was unimportant to me.

I guess Joey picked up on what I was thinking. I've since had the feeling that he could read people as easily as I could, that he could sense things about others that they didn't know themselves.

"A helluva place to get introduced," he quipped, the sunny smile still on his lips. He reached into his breast pocket and pulled out a business card. "Why don't you come by the office one day, Officer—" he paused to read my name tag—"Bell. We could have lunch, talk."

It was my turn to grin. I pulled out my pen and quickly wrote out a speeding ticket. Tearing it off, I handed it to Joey, "Give this to your driver, and tell him this is a 45-mile-per-hour zone. He was traveling 48. That's breaking the law."

He laughed and took the ticket. "Sure, sure" he said, slipping the business card into my palm. A big double-loaded rig came roaring by. Deafening sound engulfed us as we looked through the billowing dust at each other. Joey never stopped smiling.

CHAPTER FOUR

A Bottle of Port

Darlene and I were married shortly after my graduation from the police academy. It was a small ceremony, and my parents came down for a modest celebration. It is one of the few fond memories I have of our time together.

Darlene was a good and loving mate, but from the beginning our marriage was under a cloud. Despite my best intentions, I couldn't help but feel some resentment over the circumstances that had forced us together before either of us was really ready to marry. In many ways, during that first year, I was a complete stranger to Darlene, and she to me. That's to be expected, I guess, yet Darlene's womanly intuition told her that her husband was unhappy. She blamed it on my job and let it be known that she expected more of me than just being a policeman. She seemed to be giving voice to my own discontent.

Although I could hardly admit it to myself, I was rapidly becoming disillusioned with police work. It was still adventurous and exciting, but there was little intellectual stimulation; many of my duties were just grinding routines. Coupled with the sordid picture I was getting of humanity and my desire for a position that matched my own self-image, I began to take a second look at being a cop.

Certainly there were no lack of intelligent fellow officers, if it was mental stimulation I lacked. Nor were the pressures and strains I experienced any more severe than those which the average rookie encounters in his first year. Law enforcement has just as much opportunity for advancement as any other career; I was even told at the time I resigned that I was seen as an excellent choice for promotion as a career officer. I could go straight to the top if I was diligent and patient. None of this, however, made much of an impression on me. No, I had dug a hole for myself and was blaming the job for putting me there. I didn't know then that the only way I could have gotten to the bottom of that pit was to have climbed in myself. The truth of it was that I had found another occupation, which was going to keep me busy for a long time to come.

It started in earnest during my rookie year. The baby had come—a beautiful healthy little girl whom we named Jerri. Darlene was working days and I took on graveyard and swing shifts to care for the infant while she was away. It was during those balmy, desert days, alone in the house, with the bright sun and chirping birds caroling the real world outside the window, that I began a long journey. I would return years later, hanging to life by a single thread.

The need grew within me at an incredible rate: within a few months I had crossed that invisible line between life and death. There were a million excuses but not a single valid one. I did it because I loved it; it was not job stress, or an unhappy childhood, or a stern father, or a deep-rooted trauma. I wanted it and would never be denied. In medical terms I had an actual allergic reaction. I want more and more, forever more. I had lost the power to choose, lost it very early. For me there was only one way to go, and I went willingly.

It was as if I had been born to the life. With blinding speed every responsibility, every facet of pride, every dream and ambition was reduced to dim memories viewed through the wrong end of a telescope. What did I care about establishing myself, finding my place in the world? I had already found it—inside a bottle.

As my addiction to alcohol grew, the real things of my life fell away. I began calling in sick to work. I was, in fact, ill much of the time. I went quickly through our meager savings and began dipping into household money to buy the stuff. I quickly came to the realization that I couldn't afford to keep up my habit on hard liquor—it was just too expensive. Although it brought with it the vilest hangovers. I found that cheap red wine got me where I needed to be the fastest and cheapest. It was a trick I picked up from the derelict wrecks whom I had hauled off to the drunk tanks periodically. If it was good enough for them . . . .

I can only guess at what went through Darlene's mind, the fears and insecurities that must have plagued her. But she had other, more immediate problems: could she safely leave little Jerri with me?

I sometimes wonder how that child survived its first years. As an infant she spent the earliest months of her young life with me, wide-eyed and innocent, an unknowing observer. When I was conscious I would care for her as best I could, but I shudder when I think of how many times I might have dropped her from my numb, fumbling fingers, snuffed out her existence by leaving a cigarette burning at the edge of her crib, or crushed the breath from her by rolling over in a drunken stupor while she lay sleeping beside me on the bed.

More often than not I would pass out, awakened hours later by the sound of her piteous cries, staring from her playpen at my motionless body on the couch, her eyes red from crying. In these times I too would start to cry, unable to believe what was happening to me and unable to do a thing about it. I talked to her for hours, and for hours more would leave her alone in her crib while I made my way to the liquor store. She was my companion, my drinking buddy—but of course no friend ever treated another as I treated her. If I thought about it at all, I guess I thought I was being a real father to her, letting her in on my problems, treating her as an equal. It was part of a pattern of justification that would repeat itself for years to come, and demonstrates to some small degree the debilitating mental effects of drinking upon an alcoholic like myself.

To think that I actually believed I was doing the child good with my self-pitying sobs, to think that somehow we were growing closer or that she understood even dimly what was happening to her father, is drunken arrogance at its height.

I've been classified (by people who know) as a "solitary drinker." I suppose in a sense that's what I am; I never went to bars or hung out in those early days with others like myself. In another sense, though, I wasn't alone at all; I had a friend, and sometimes I wonder if she still bears the scars of my "companionship."

How can I explain the transition that took place in those fateful months? The seeds may have been planted long before, but how had the straggling vine sprung up so quickly and taken such deep root? I can look back on my days in the Air Force, or even further, to high school, when on occasion I would drink heavily. Once or twice I even remember others, my mom or a close friend, commenting on it, but certainly no one could have anticipated this plunge into uncontrollable obsession, and in as short a time as I accomplished it. I couldn't even see what was staring me in the eye until a score of agonizing years later. What then is the explanation? How could Gary Bell, a man at the threshold of his life, have fallen so easily, so blindly, so *willingly* into this deadly embrace?

Whatever the psychological, medical, or technical reasons, I drank because I loved to drink—loved it more than life itself. There is no reason for that, no equation long or short that can explain it away, no mitigating circumstance to excuse it, and only one thing I know of to overcome it. Sitting in a sunlit room on an early afternoon, a bottle clutched in my arms as an infant girl cried for food, I was light years away from finding that answer.

CHAPTER
FIVE

Dorothy

Darlene and I, trying to secure the tenuous moorings of our future, decided that it would be best for me to quit the police force. It was a delusion, of course. She was telling me that the strain was beginning to show, that I wasn't suited for a blue-collar job, and I was thinking desperately that it was the work that brought on the boozing. Everything for me was subject now to two basic and opposing forces: my need to drink and my fear of what it was doing to me. I convinced myself that a change of occupation was just what I needed to get a fresh start.

Yet even as these words were going around in my mind, another part of me was craving the next swig of port wine. I had begun, involuntarily, to establish the classic behavior pattern of an alcohol addict: hiding my drinking from my wife and friends, taking my doses on the sly, stashing bottles around the house, and running out to the store on the slightest pretext and downing a bottle or two on the way home.

My tolerance to booze was, by any measure, amazing. As a result, I was forced to sneak around continually, nipping here and there, in constant fear of discovery. I held myself in delicate mental balance in those days, like a high-wire performer whose right foot doesn't know what his left is doing. One half of me was convinced that if I just got a good break, if someone in the right position would recognize my natural abilities, then my nightmare would vanish like the morning mist. The other half, of course, shrieked and raged for more booze, twisting like a knife in my veins until I answered the call. The tension of living out this double purpose gave me even more reason to drink. Escaping tension was one more car in the self-justifying house of cards I was building.

A friend of Darlene's was working as a secretary for a large Southwestern bank and trust company. Through her connections there, she secured me a job as a collection officer. "Collection officer" was really a euphemistic term for someone who extracted bad debts owed the bank.

Shortly after my resignation from the police force, at a time when things seemed to be pulling themselves together, my mother died of lung cancer. It was a tremendous blow to me, yet I was able to bury much of my sorrow by making arrangements for the funeral and by caring for my father. They had both been living in Phoenix, and with her gone he needed someone nearby to look after his needs and keep away loneliness. My work at the bank was tolerable; I was able to hide the worst effects of my secret drinking and did an admirable job with my unpleasant assignments. I felt I could fairly ask the bank for a transfer to Phoenix, to be closer to my father, and they graciously complied.

Despite the very real sorrow which I suffered at the loss of my mother, the move to Phoenix seemed especially favorable, and I was grateful for the chance to relocate to a new job and a new environment. Now I was away from the cramped apartment, stifling with the memories of drunkenness and remorse, away from Tucson, the scene of so many sordid, petty crimes, so many abused and hapless victims. Surely if anyone was being offered a new chance, it was Gary Bell. I longed for the opportunity to wipe the tarnish from my self-image.

Unfortunately, my work at the bank proved not much more elevating than law enforcement. Occasionally I would come across a real hard-luck case, people who had defaulted on their bank loans for any number of unfortunate reasons. Most of the time, however, it was the deadbeats, the hucksters, and the fast operators whose schemes had caught up with them, or, as was more often the case, people who never intended paying back the bank in the first place. Repossessing cars, furniture, or real estate from these people never kept me awake at night. They were just a notch above the street hoods and con artists I had had to deal with as a policeman. I wore a suit and represented a bank, and some of the more repugnant elements were gone, such as the batterings and the bloody deaths, but it still seemed a demeaning way to make a living, with even less chance of meeting people who weren't on the down side of life.

It was all just more grist for my mill—more reason for me to drink, and in drinking to rail against the fates for the bad turns my life was taking.

Darlene, Jerri, and I moved in with my dad, into his comfortable spacious house in suburban Phoenix. It seemed ideal at first, just the change we all needed. I took my work seriously and by all accounts was very good at it. But behind this cheerful facade the pressures of my double life were beginning to wear away the mask. It was, of course, foolish to think that a change of scene and a new job would affect in any way the rot which was eating away at the roots of

my life. I continued to drink, perhaps a bit more sur-
reptitiously than in those dreadful days in Tucson
alone with Jerri, but nevertheless consistently and
heavily. Darlene was working again, and we hired a
sitter for Jerri. As a collector, traveling around from
delinquent account to delinquent account, I had an
almost-entirely free rein to indulge my limitless thirst.
The tightrope I walked was getting narrower all the
time, and my feet ever more uncertain.

What I was initially able to hide from my
superiors at the bank I was unable to keep from
Darlene and my father. Although it hurt me almost
unbearably to see the look in my dad's eyes as he
slowly came to realize what was happening to his
son, there was nothing I could do or was willing to
do about it. I raided his liquor cabinet with the
same disregard that I wrote bad checks at every
store in the neighborhood. I tried desperately to
cover, with my salary and Darlene's as well as with
loans from my dad, what was becoming an increasingly expensive habit. Even drinking the cheapest
port wine, I ran up bills that seriously threatened
our financial security. I found myself sinking
further and further into an abyss of self-pity.
Weekends would find me, on the pretext of making
collections, driving around with Jerri, with a bottle
in my lap, visiting all the spots my mother and I
had seen during that first visit to Phoenix—eons
ago, it now seemed. I would weep shamelessly,
blurting out my problems to her ghost, taking a
maudlin enjoyment in my miserable condition.

It was only a matter of time before my excesses
caught up to me at the job. I began getting warnings
from my superiors. My work was falling off as I
spent increasing on-the-job hours in shady
downtown bars, pushing back impending disaster
with each belt. My glib manner and winning per-

sonality were starting to fail me and my bosses were beginning to see the threadbare reality of this aggressive young opportunist they had taken on. The guise of my upwardly mobile ambitions were less than adequate to cover the plummeting dive I was taking into the bottle. It was around then, I guess, that I crossed another invisible line: from being a daily drinker to being a periodic drinker. By this I mean that I wouldn't drink every day, but when I did drink it was for extended periods of heavy use. At first these episodes were two or three months apart. Eventually, however, they began drawing closer and closer together. The chinks in my armor of self-respect were becoming wide, vulnerable gaps.

Home life, under the reproachful eyes of my father, was becoming unbearable. Darlene and I, now clutching at straws, decided that we would be better off finding our own home. It was the blind hope of one more false start. A real-estate-agent friend found a charming little place not far from my dad, and, scraping together the down payment, we made the move.

A short period of well-being followed, but our words of assurance to each other sounded more and more hollow as the specter of my alcoholism loomed larger. Darlene pleaded and cajoled, using every means at her disposal in a futile attempt to slow me down. It was useless. Knowing full well how she felt—she had laid down the law in our new home: no booze in the house—I simply took to more and more devious subterfuges to get my daily dose. I hid a bottle in the tank of the bathroom commode, in the cushions of the sofa, at the bottom of the clothes hamper. I even took to pouring out bottles of disinfectant and refilling them with liquor.

It was all terribly clever, this hideous game of hide and seek, I thought at the time. But of course it's an age-old tragedy, played out across history and around the world, wherever and whenever the demon strikes. When a human being has to have it, there is no humiliation, no deception, no cruelty to which he or she will not stoop. Ask the tired and broken prostitutes walking the streets; ask the wretched derelict sleeping in the garbage; ask the man who has lost everything but that burning need . . . ask me. It doesn't matter what it may be; just name your poison—booze, drugs, money, influence. Whenever the lust for these things supersedes the tenets of basic human dignity, how a man treats himself and others, the result is always the same: dehumanization. The clever charades, the ruses and deceptions I practiced on Darlene in order to have what I craved is the single most scathing indictment of how much I esteemed our marriage.

We weren't, I guess you could say, meant for each other to begin with. We would probably have had a rough time of it under the best of circumstances. The basic differences in our personalities and backgrounds were working against us. Not more love, nor more patience, nor more understanding from my wife could have cured me. In short, *no* amount of human kindness would have reached me then, or for a long time to come.

When I think of Darlene these days, I sometimes wonder how she endured as much as she did. It wasn't as if she had no idea of the ravages of alcohol on the human psyche. Her own father had been a particularly heavy and abusive drinker, a man who, when in his cups, took malicious pleasure in raging through the house, breaking up the furniture and shouting imprecations. He owned two large and vicious hound dogs which he used for hunting, and he would often threaten to sic the animals on Darlene's mother. As a young girl, she had grown up in an atmosphere of constant fear and tension. Had she simply blinded herself to my condition, choosing to forget memories that must have caused her deep pain? Or was it that she saw in me something worth clinging to at any cost? Her answers to those questions might be more than I could bear to hear.

Even in the life of a committed alcoholic, the wheels which grind out fortune's way spin in different directions. While I sank further and further into my self-consuming inferno, other logs were turning, bringing new people into my life and old "friends" back on the scene. One particular day at the bank, the elements of life and death were brought into even closer proximity.

It couldn't have been more than a few months after moving to Phoenix, and I hadn't yet assumed my duties as a collection officer. They had temporarily put me behind the counter as a teller. I didn't think much of the job; in the hierarchy of banking institutions, just about anything is more prestigious than being a teller. But I quietly endured it because I knew that as soon as a permanent replacement could be found, I'd be out collecting.

Just before lunch that day, the bank manager brought the new teller. "Gary," he said, "I'd like you to meet Dorothy. She'll be taking over for you, and I'd like you to give her the benefit of your experience. Dorothy," he said, turning to the replacement, "Gary here will be showing you the ropes over the next few weeks." He paused while we shook hands, "I'll leave you to it, then," he said, and returned to his desk.

A petite, attractive young woman with rich auburn hair and frank blue eyes regarded me. A slight smile conveyed her sense of expectation. I can't say that I felt equal to those appraising eyes, embroiled as I was in my own convoluted web of problems, but I summoned up what reserves of charm I could to return the smile. I was immediately attracted to her (in all the wrong ways, naturally), yet there was something about her straightforward manner, the calm and self-possessed way she carried herself, that made me feel a little intimidated.

Anybody whose world is crumbling about his ears, as mine was, might have felt the same way in that moment, looking into those eyes, smelling the clean smell of her hair and clothes and feeling her vitality radiating like the warming touch of the sun. I felt small next to her, a little grubby and most definitely sorry for myself. My problems were more than a confident and well-bred lady like this could ever hope to understand. What could she know about the misery of my home life, my terrifying tightrope walk? Yet even as I thought these things, I found myself wanting very much to tell her everything.

We had lunch together that day, and I found to my surprise that I could open up easily to this remarkable young woman. Maybe it was just self-pity, the need to spill the whole sordid sequence of my life out to someone. Maybe I was motivated more by the simple desire to get closer to her; any way I could I wanted to make points with Dorothy, and I colored my story to suit the situation, though never throwing caution entirely to the wind. I told her that Darlene didn't understand me, that my true abilities were being wasted, and a few other absurdly embellished facts. I wanted, I needed to have this girl on my side. Don't ask me why, but I just took to her—how she carried herself, her dress, the way she wore her hair, plus a million small details that added up to a bit of class that was sorely missing from my daily grind.

If Dorothy was surprised or shocked to hear such intimate, if doctored, details about a total stranger, she didn't let on. Rather, she was open and receptive in a way that I could hardly believe. My estimation of a protected, cultured, and aloof young lady melted before her very real concern and sympathy. There was a compassion and warmth about her that drew me strongly on. I *wanted* to tell her more, I wanted to tell her everything—the real truth.

Even if I couldn't summon up the courage that afternoon, over our long lunch, the sense of trust, of knowing that I could reveal more to her than to anyone I knew, gave me a sense of comfort. It was a good feeling that couldn't be supplanted by the cocktails I downed while I spun my fabricated history. If it had been up to me, I would have taken her straight to the nearest motel after lunch, for even in the midst of these ennobling sensations my alter ego was working full-time. But the opportunity did not and could not present itself. Dorothy was not that kind of woman, I told myself, and the thought was comforting.

Late that afternoon I was in the teller's cage, counting and stacking bills prior to the close of business. As I made my final tally I heard someone come up to the window.

"I'm sorry," I said, without looking up from my work. "This window is closed."

"Even for a pal, Gary?" replied a familiar voice, and, looking up I was caught easily in the smiling eyes of Joey.

CHAPTER SIX

Joey

Joey was interested in me. Always had been. We had met a few more times in Tucson while I was on the police force, and each time he had offered me a place in his organization. I laughed at his enticements back then; the whole idea of working for the Mafia was something that happened in books—it was too farfetched to take seriously. Of course I knew that the mob was very real and every bit as vicious and widespread as the popular legend had it. Through my police work I had learned a lot about their actual operations, but the thought of big-time crime as a career move, what with a wife and a kid and not so much as a shoplifting conviction on my record, seemed completely absurd.

Nevertheless, Joey was completely serious about his offers. What he promised even in general terms—money, power, and women—were not the kind of subjects he took lightly. He made no pretense about it. He had found a kindred spirit even if I hadn't recognized the fact. He played on my dissatisfaction with law enforcement, assuring me that the life he was offering was everything I'd ever wanted. There is no doubt that Joey was an astute judge of character; he recognized things in me that I hadn't any inkling of, and he was right: capacities for violence, intimidation, and cruelty; unknown cravings and appetites, frightening capabilities. Back then, with my idealism and self-confidence still intact, I could afford to play along for the laughs, pretending that I was ready to switch sides when he made the right offer. But when he walked into that bank to open an account, I wasn't laughing.

A short time before our accidental encounter, Joey had moved to Phoenix to open his own nightclub. It was located on the outskirts of town, and we went there after work to talk things over and have a few drinks. He was as smooth and genteel as ever, full of good cheer as he told me how exciting it was to have his own place. It was going to be the hottest spot in the Southwest, he boasted, and he wanted to let me in on the ground floor. It was the old game again, but this time I found myself a little more eager to play.

Downing one cocktail after another while a happy crowd swirled around us, I began toying with the idea of making real money, to be able to dress and carry myself like Joey. Although I felt every bit his equal as far as brains and personality went, I had to admit, if only to myself, that he had gone considerably farther in life than I had. He walked in a world of adventure and danger that looked pretty good to me just about then. Working as a collection officer, grappling with my drinking demon, and facing a disintegrating home life and a crippled self-image, I liked the idea of calling the shots.

There was something else I liked about Joey—he didn't seem to care, or even notice, how much I was drinking that night or any of the other evenings we spent at his club. I was careful not to reveal the full extent of my addiction, but I certainly went as far as I could without losing control, far enough for anyone to see that I could put away the sauce. I'm sure Joey noticed, but he never said a word and never once suggested that I'd have to clean up my act in order to accept his offer. It was a real difference from the straight-laced, bureaucratic bank officials, who were always handing out warnings and watching me like a hawk for any signs of ineptitude. Obviously it had to do with the nature of the jobs; financial institutions required sobriety from their employees in every sense of the word, while Joey wanted a completely different set of personality traits.

Yet even in my wildest drunken fancies I couldn't seriously entertain the idea of hooking up with Joey's little business concern. I had a job, I told myself. I had a wife and a daughter and house payments and a list of woes as long as my arm. The mob was strictly for hard-core cases, and I sure wasn't one of them. Not yet.

Darlene knew nothing of Joey and his offers. She was also ignorant of another developing relationship in my life, one that was to have an even more profound effect on my future, although at the time it was just another desperate secret from that hidden part of my life.

Questions of love are tricky at best. A case could certainly be made for the love Darlene and I shared during our courtship, such as it was. I loved my father, and Jerri and of course the bottle. But there are some kinds of love that, by their very nature, are different. Often such a love is against our better judgment and against the models we would set for our lives.

It's a fact that applied with equal force to both Dorothy and myself, although perhaps more for her. True, there were reasons for what she did, for the way she turned against what she so strongly believed, but the real reason had nothing to do with circumstances or the passion of the moment. It was that other, mysterious factor, that fateful sense of destiny—a destiny that would not bear its fruit for many years to come. Yet somewhere in the secret heart that motivates us all, I believe we both knew from the first that we would stay together.

From childhood, Dorothy had been a believing Christian. I say "believing" because it was not just cultural conditioning or traditional imperative that sparked her faith. It was a real commitment to a God that moved in very real ways in her life. She went regularly to church and was an active member. She studied the Bible and prayed with a simple but real faith. All of this makes what happened that much more inexplicable.

When I first met Dorothy in the bank, she had been married for a few years to a man named John, a clerk in a hardware store. I suppose at the time I must have felt some contempt for John, satisfied as he was in his menial job, serving up nuts and bolts and never dreaming about something better. I begrudged him Dorothy, telling myself that she deserved something better, a man with some ambition.

Dorothy told me at lunch one day that her husband had tuberculosis. It seemed that she too had secrets to tell, secrets that she dealt with as honestly as she could, but that nonetheless were taking a toll on her happiness. I'll never forget the moment when, taking full stock of me with her eyes, she revealed that she had not been sleeping regularly with her husband. The disease, she explained, had left him not only frail and sickly but almost impotent.

It was a revelation with implications that did not escape me; suddenly all the undercurrents that I had suppressed from our first meeting began surfacing, as possibilities sprung unbidden from deep within us both. She must know, I thought, what this confession meant. No longer were we just co-workers, sharing an occasional coffee break or lunch together. No longer was I alone in my wistful imaginings about how things might be between us. She had as much as told me that she too imagined our friendship as a way out, a way to escape, to catch something of her fleeting young womanhood.

Others, I suppose, would question the faith of anyone who abandoned herself to the passions of the moment, as Dorothy did. She was, after all, a married woman, and no matter how desperate the situation might have been, God's grace would be sufficient. I guess there really is no argument in response to such a case; she was a Christian, and as such she had willingly violated one of the central tenets of her religion—the sanctity of marriage. Far be it from me to try to defend her or what she did. For my part, I am probably less culpable; I didn't have a creed to constrain me. I took advantage of the opportunity offered with a relish born from my own desires and all the conditioning of the American male.

All I can say is this: the God that Dorothy believed in so fervently, and the faith that sustained her even as guilt threatened to overwhelm, do indeed work all things to good for those who believe. If you have any concept of sin, then the illicit sexual liaison that Dorothy and I plunged so thoughtlessly into was indeed a sin. But I put it to you this way: without that sin and the way that sin was turned to good, I would be a dead man right now.

Dorothy and I had been set apart for something very special; I needed her as much as she needed me. Sometimes the neatly tied ends of people's lives are left unrevealed for a long, long time. Dorothy and I were allowed to see the end result of our chance meeting in the bank, and what looked to all the world like tragedy was eventually turned to triumph.

Like Darlene before her, Dorothy was left with the burden of our love affair. Our furtive meetings and their consummating moments had their inevitable results. This time, however, all my misplaced good intentions could do nothing. There was no way I could offer marriage, no way I could pretend to provide for the child I had planted. To be fair Dorothy never expected it of me. Her guilt was something she bore alone; her shame was a fact she held in her arms, nurtured, and called her daughter. Those who might feel that such sufferings are the wages of sin will get no argument from me. Again, I just point to the facts. Janet, my second daughter, was the child born out of sin, and yet a more lively, happy, and beautiful child would have been hard to find.

This information, of course, I know only through Dorothy. I wasn't there to hold her hand, bring her flowers, and coo over the infant. I was at home with Darlene and Jerri, keeping up the charade of my foolish pride, pretending, pretending . . . .

The joys of parenthood were left instead to John, of whose justifications and self-evasions I can only guess. He certainly must have known that the child was not his own, and could have attributed nothing less than a miracle to its birth if he was to assume the rights of fatherhood. Yet assume them he did. From the very beginning, Janet bore a strong resemblance to me, and in any case I was really the only possible candidate for papa. What a fool, I thought at the time, when Dorothy had told me of John's willingness to ask no questions and be told no lies.

Yet now I think something much different when my mind turns to that pallid clerk in the hardware store. Certainly, whatever his reasons were for accepting Dorothy and the child, he must in his own secret moments have known something of the truth. Perhaps he loved Dorothy, perhaps a child *was* something close to a miracle to him, regardless of whose it was. Perhaps he knew a way to forgiveness that eludes most of us, and even if he raised that child in total ignorance of the truth, I can only thank him for sticking by Dorothy and our child, providing a home for them, putting food on the table and clothes on their backs.

It was shortly after Dorothy left the bank on pregnancy leave that I stopped seeing her altogether. I suppose I might have missed her, wondered what was happening to her, and how she was holding up. I might have even thought after the child, missed its sweet scent, its kicks and squirms beneath the swaddling clothes. I might have missed all of it, but to tell you the truth I don't remember. All my time and energy was taken up with another love, one that demanded everything. And got it.

CHAPTER SEVEN

"You're Sick, Mr. Bell"

Slowly but surely, booze was draining me of my last vestiges of dignity. With each successive binge I became more subjugated. I thought nothing of lying to Darlene, creating elaborate excuses to cover the time I spent furtively maintaining my high. Homelife, and with it a decent environment for Jerri—a place of security and nurturing for the young child—had vanished. The guilt and recriminations, the arguing and pleading between Darlene and me grew increasingly bitter. My wife was coming to the end of her rope as she realized that nothing could help me.

She began threatening to leave, to take Jerri and clear out for good, abandoning me to stew in my own juice. If I was drunk at these times I would rail against her, cursing and screaming, pushing myself to the edge of hysteria and actual violence. But when I was hung over I was invariably remorseful, full of crocodile tears and empty promises. I was actually very much afraid of losing my family; Jerri was especially precious to me even as I lost my grip on everything else. I had pretty much seen her through infancy, for better or worse; I had changed her diapers and talked endlessly to her, or rather at her, about the hard deal I was getting from life. She was my little girl.

There is something tragic about the face of children whose few years are filled with uncertainty and fear, who listen wide-awake as their parents, the guardians of their minds and bodies, scream hopelessly at each other, shattering the home and the heart of the innocent victim with each shout and every hurled insult. Yet, like a drunken high-wire artist, with each step more erratic and each movement wilder and more spasmed, I was balanced precariously over the abyss, unable and unwilling to consider the consequences of the fall for myself or my daughter.

That fall came with the inevitability of gravity, and with it came an even blacker night, a more profound blindness, than I could ever have imagined. A circle of destruction encompassed me as my madness took on new and horrifying dimensions. And it was not just for myself and my family, nor just for those others who trusted me at a job, nor just for the increasingly small group of friends who suffered for me; soon complete strangers would fall helpless in this wake of desolation.

After less than a year-and-a half I failed at my second aborted career attempt. I lost my job at the bank, quitting before they had a chance to fire me. I pretended again that I wasn't suited for the work, that better things were in store for me, more lucrative opportunities. It was a desperate sham, a wild twist of logic to keep me balanced on the thin line between hope and complete abandonment.

It must have been a real relief for the bank managers not to have to witness my bleary, trembling arrival at the bank most mornings, wondering how long it would be before I made a serious mistake at their expense. It had been a trying year-and-a-half for everyone; the hopeful new beginning signaled by our move to Phoenix had turned into a sour nightmare, our ambitious resolve returning to mock us. Darlene talked more than ever of leaving with Jerri while I sank into an insensible numbness.

My next shot at a job was selling home food freezers. I lasted an entire day and sold not a single appliance. I think that was the beginning of the end for me in terms of really even caring. I sat at home and drank for days now, even weeks at a time, passing in and out of consciousness, dreaming dreams that floated away on the fumes of cheap wine, making promises to myself, my dad, my wife, the empty air, forgetting what I had said minutes later.

I was no longer that aggressive, highly motivated young boy, winning the playground battles. I was no longer that sharp, success-oriented achiever, eager for a chance to carve his niche. I was no longer a father or a husband, no longer a man capable of caring about himself, whether sick or well, happy or sad, alive or dead. I was no longer even human. I was being swallowed whole by darkness, turning head over heels in a vacuum where no voice or touch could reach me. My balancing act had failed. There were no longer two sides of my life; there was nothing to reconcile, no image to maintain. I was an alcoholic.

When Darlene came home from work that day, she found me crawling around the kitchen floor on all fours, whimpering and slobbering like a beaten dog. I had completely lost control. How she got me into the car I'll never know, nor do I know what she said to our family doctor, or how they had admitted the raving, uncontrollable animal that I had become into a hospital for "acute gastritis."

I was taken to a small, khaki-green admitting room while Darlene and my dad, who had also been summoned, waited anxiously outside. The room was full of what looked to me like wicked instruments of torture—standard emergency-room equipment. I felt cold, utterly alone and terrified, as something of my actual condition was beginning to dawn on me. It seemed like hours that I spent there by myself, watching the walls swim before my eyes as slowly the awareness of pain began to spread upwards from my abdomen. Eventually a nurse arrived and ordered me to get undressed. She left, and hours more of real or imagined time passed as I fought to free myself from the leaden weight of my pants, shoes, and shirt.

At last I was sitting naked, weak, and shivering on the edge of the examining table beneath the harsh neon light. It was a moment of total vulner- ability—no booze to escape into, no family to comfort me. I was naked and exposed in a hostile world. Around me chrome and tile glistened, and glaring light bounced off the shining surfaces and into my eyes. And all the while an agony was building in my gut. I needed a drink.

But there was none to be had. There were only sharp wrenching sensations up through my spine and into my brain. I began to cough, shivering violently now, hacking against a hard knot that was concentrating in my stomach. Harder and harder I coughed, until the cough grew into wracking fits as my body shook like an Autumn leaf. I was doubled over, clutching my midsection, my sweat-covered brow resting on my knees. Still the coughing continued. Then with a sudden force I vomited, splattering the acrid fluid over myself and the floor.

The stinging taste brought a shock that jolted me into a new awareness. The convulsing nausea threatened to overwhelm me. I vomited a second time, and a third time, trying weakly to call for help but unable to utter a single sound other than a low groan which seemed to come from the very center of the pain. I opened my eyes to the blinding brightness and looked at my shuddering legs, soaked and stinking. I could feel the trails of fluid running down my calves and saw for the first time the bits of dark red matter, like pieces of meat, all around me in the pool I had made. I quaked with fear and pain; I was dying, throwing up my own stomach, tearing myself apart, piece by quivering piece. I couldn't stop vomiting; the lacerating anguish had moved into my chest as I fell to the floor, my face pressed into the stench.

When I woke again I was in a long, narrow bed. My feet beneath the covers seemed miles away. There was a strange sense of disembodiment brought on by the heavy exhaustion which lay across me like a weight. I wanted to sleep, to pass into the night for a thousand years, but my mind would not rest; thoughts seemed to possess a life of their own, turning over and over like lunatic acrobats, chaotic and out of sync. A doctor, his thin, craggy features reflecting only professional concern, came and leaned close into my face, filling my vision. Fear, rising like the nausea, gave me new energy: fear of his voice, fear of what he might do to me—unreasoning, bestial fear. I wondered how long it would be before I could have a drink. I needed something familiar in this alien place full of smells, strangers, and pain.

As the doctor was talking, more people came into the room, including Darlene. She spoke, but, like the doctor, I couldn't understand the sound that was coming from her mouth. I tried to follow her lips, but my eyes swam. My mind, raging beyond its limits, couldn't slow things down enough to make sense of them. The doctor extended long fingers, each vein and knotty joint standing out in sharp relief. I cringed, a whimper escaping from deep inside, as I felt him moving over my belly, his fingers prodding and poking. Other doctors and a nurse stood by and watched. Darlene had disappeared from my view. Suddenly his grasping digits found their mark; a well of pain, a large swollen area, outlined its shape in throbbing agony. A fresh sweat sprang up on my forehead while my hands clutched the bedsheets.

Questions were asked, exchanges made. Everything was spoken in low, confidential tones, and then, as suddenly as they had come, all the people left and the room was empty. Once again I was alone with the pain. I waited while somewhere soundless seconds ticked by. I had no idea of the time, of where I was, or why I still needed a drink, but at the moment the physical pain was far worse than the thirst. I knew something was happening deep inside me. My body was reacting at long last, rebelling against the tyranny of alcohol. It was at war with me, fighting for its own survival, calling on the dumb instinct to live, to keep on breathing.

Three years of heavy drinking, the last few months of which were unrelenting, had finally been collected in a brutal, knifing ache. If I could have ripped the damage from me in that moment, torn out a hideously swollen liver and my bleeding stomach, I would have done it. As it was, my body was accomplishing much the same thing.

A door opened and a nurse came in, an old black woman whose skin gleamed next to the starched white of her uniform. Her eyes burned as she came closer to the bed and laughed a wicked laugh. She stood close to me, smoothing the sheets with her burnished hands and speaking in a slow, distinct voice. Every word was clear, as if she were talking to some calm center of my mind, still functioning beneath the onslaught of pain.

"You sick, Mr. Bell," she crooned, "You very, very sick. They say you goin' to die." It was as if she were singing a soft lullaby to me, her voice husky and full. "They say you gonna cough you'self to death, Mr. Bell. They say you gonna cough you' liver right out of you' mouth." She turned to the bedstand and opened the drawer. "They say the booze is gonna kill you, Mr. Bell." she whispered, lifting a hypodermic needle into the light and squirting a few sparkling drops into the air. "They say you' already half dead." She leaned closer, her white teeth showing, her eyes searing deeper and deeper. I screamed and another jolt shivered up my spine. Shouting an unintelligible sound, I struck out at her.

Still smiling, she disappeared into thin air.

CHAPTER EIGHT

The Little Yellow Eyes

When I awoke again the pain was gone. I felt a little lightheaded, but I was thinking clearly for what seemed like the first time in days. How much time had passed? I wondered. Was it day or night? I turned in the bed, which was wider now and not so hard. A large window next to me announced late afternoon, and I could see the street stretching out into the clear Southwestern afternoon. Was it cold or warm out there? I mused to myself.

For the first time I realized that I hadn't the faintest idea what season it was. The month and day of the week were a complete mystery to me. All I knew for sure was what I could see out that window. The waning day, the colors of the sky, the gentle sloping road that led into a tree-lined residential neighborhood—all seem peaceful and calm. Somewhere a dog barked and a bird caroled the day's end with a few sharp notes.

The person in the bed next to mine stirred, turned his head to me, and smiled. His name was George; he was just out of an appendix operation and would be laid up for the next couple of days. Too bad, he said; it was the best time for business, and he couldn't really afford it, but what are you gonna do . . . .

We talked together for awhile, and I was completely open and honest, telling him I was there for drinking, that I had been very sick but was feeling much better. It was good to talk to this genial stranger. I felt free to be candid for the first time in as long as I could remember. For a few moments I even sensed a little of my old ease and self-assurance returning. We exchanged pleasantries for awhile. He asked me if I wanted something to eat, that he wasn't allowed to but that this shouldn't stop me from eating.

It was then that I noticed that the place where my stomach should be was just a large empty sensation, or rather a lack of sensation. There was no aching, no growling for nourishment—just a deadened part. Strange, I thought to myself, and mentally took stock of the rest of my body. It all seemed to be there—everything but my abdomen. While George droned on, I lifted up the bedsheets and my hosptial gown to have a look. What I saw was not a hole, but a large discolored area, like a bruise, across my midsection. I stared at it uncomprehendingly, and as I did it started to move writhing as the colors shifted and changed beneath the flesh. In sudden horror I threw down the sheets and slid further down into the bed. My God, I thought, what have I done to myself?

Then I heard the sounds. They came from a long way off at first, then got louder and more distinct every moment. Shouting and singing, hoots and laughter, sounds like a trundling circus procession, drifted up the quiet street. I looked out the window, telling George to watch for the parade.

Moments passed as I strained to make out the noises coming nearer. every once in a while I could just catch what was being said or shouted. It puzzled me to think that Darlene and my father were marching in this parade. I heard their voices distinctly from around a bend in the road, calling to me in a strange echoing tone with singsong rhymes.

Finally, in a flourish of color and noise, the cacophony emerged into view. Leading the procession was a full-bore brass marching band. Their red-and-gold uniforms glinted in the waning sun, the sight far surpassing any marching band I had ever seen before. The trumpets and cornets blared a dissonant, unearthly tune, while a full battery of bass drums, snares, and tom-toms beat out the lopsided rhythm. Majorettes pirouetted down the avenue, throwing batons high in the air, twirling like tops in their short, frilly skirts and white boots. An honor guard bore huge unfurling flags, while an escort of motorcycle cops performed manuevers on growling black bikes. Behind them, in perfectly symmetrical formation, were soldiers—First World War doughboys in wide-brimmed hats and leather legging. They filled the street, singing that same off-key melody.

It was an amazing sight. I watched with fascination, exclaiming to my roommate every few moments at what I was seeing. George had stopped talking—I assumed he was also watching the wonders unfolding out the window.

The marching band and rows of soldiers passed, and there was a slight pause while other sounds could be heard coming closer. Then, from around the corner, on bicycles and roller skates, in convertibles and antique autos, perched on running boards and gunning motorcycle engines, came the entire cast of characters of Gary Bell's life. It seemed that everyone I knew or had known, living or dead, was coming down the street past the window. It wasn't just my father and Darlene, but also my mother, riding in the back of the car and yelling up at me where I lay; old schoolmates; commanding officers from my Air Force days; battered and slack-jawed faces of suicide victims and homicide cases dredged from my worse moments as a copy; the two lieutenants and the captain who had grilled me so mercilessly; the faces of customers and foreclosure victims I had known from the bank; Joey; my highschool football team; the doctor who had examined me—all jumbled together in that mob of moving wheels, all passing by and calling up with the same tinny voices, each singing a little ditty, a poem of rhyming verse.

Gary Bell, Gary Bell,
How much time have you spent in hell?
shouted my old Air Force drill sergeant.

Gary, Gary, come back soon;
Stand with us 'neath the light
of the moon.

I could make out their faces clearly through the window, some smiling up to me, others, weeping, tears flowing like opened taps down their faces. I saw Jerri, pedaling a tricycle, waving and calling up to me in her small voice—

When daddy drank from the bottle red
I cried and cried from my lonely bed
When daddy coughed he coughed so loud
They covered him with a funeral shroud.

On and on it went, this mad procession, and not once did I question the evidence of my eyes. I could hear George in the background calling for a nurse as I strained to make out what my friends and family were saying.

I'll make you an offer you can't refuse— yelled Joey, dressed impeccably as usual, but sliding down the sidewalk on roller skates.

I'll cut you free, I'll turn you loose,
I'll make them each regret the day;
When you walk by they'll all make way.

After a while I noticed that they weren't moving on with the rest of the parade, but had all come to gather under the hospital window, parking their bikes and cars and coming across the lawn to peer in through the glass. Each one of them carried something in his or her hand, and as they crowded around, all shouting and gesturing at once, I saw that they were holding rifles and pistols, which they brandished with angry, determined looks.

"Don't open the window!" I screamed above the din to George. He shook his head, a wild look in his eyes, pushing the button beside his bed and glancing nervously at the door for a nurse to arrive. It was too late. I watched with horror as the mob began climbing up past the sill to the roof. I could hear scampering footsteps above me, and I could make out their voices through the air-conditioning grates. As I watched I could see the screws which held the grates in place unscrew slowly, then more rapidly.

"No!" I shrieked. "No, please, stay out!" With a clatter the grates fell to the floor and the nightmarish figures slithered through the holes and into my room. Only now they weren't the half-forgotten faces from my past, but small agile children, each holding a weapon and dashing under my bed, behind the curtain, into the bathroom, and down the hall. They peered at me with yellow, gleaming eyes. "Come out!" I screamed at them, my fear turning to anger. "Come out and show yourselves, you little monsters! Come here and let me cut your thieving little hearts out!"

I heard a soft pop and felt a stinging on the back of my neck. I whirled around in time to see one of the dwarf-like creatures lower his gun and scramble behind a chair. Another pop and a sharp pain on my cheek. I was being fired at! Suddenly from every direction echoing pops filled the rooms. I howled in pain, thrashing helplessly in the bed, trying to move out of their aim. I could hear their high-pitched giggles, like recordings at the wrong speed, and in a rage I shouted every filthy name I could remember. The small black pellets they were firing at me were falling onto the white sheets and I started to gather them to throw back at the demons. But as I picked them up they would vanish in my hands.

Meanwhile the tiny snipers were moving closer and closer, whispering to themselves, crouching in twos and threes and advancing on the bed. I could see their smooth paces and their golden-blonde hair; only their eyes reflected the malice and hatred they had for me. When they all raised their guns at once and took careful aim at my head, I leaped from the sheets with a banshee's wail and took off down the hall, my open-backed hospital gown flapping around me.

"They're after me!" I shouted, my voice echoing down the sterile corridors. "The little people are trying to kill me!" The last thing I remember is the hands, thrust from starched white sleeves, latching onto me, holding me tight, dragging me to the floor.

When I awoke I was in another bed in another room, by myself. The light was bright in my eyes, and with a groan I tried to cover my face. That's when I discovered I had been strapped down at the wrists and ankles. A few seconds later, without warning, the pain returned.

CHAPTER NINE

Back to the Bottle

Night had fallen. I sat alone in the light of the TV as it droned out the evening news—trouble overseas, rising prices, threats and promises. I cradled a bottle of red wine in my lap, taking long swallows and thinking of nothing. Darlene was gone, I didn't know where. She had taken Jerri with her, or at least I assumed she had. But everything was okay. I had found ten dollars in the top drawer of her bureau, and I still had three bottles next to me on the sofa.

I had been out of the hospital two days now. The DT's had faded and the terrifying and incredible hallucinations had gone away. The uncontrollable shaking, as well as the cold sweats and dry heaves, had slowed down and ceased. Muscle control and speech returned, and with them remorse. I had wept with self-pity as the doctors shook their heads and told me that I had come perilously close to ending my own life. I was jaundiced and suffering from acute malnutrition, and I had given myself cirrhosis of the liver. It was, in fact, dead parts of my liver that I had been vomiting up those first few days. My ruined organ had become so large that it protruded from where my stomach should have been. The infection was so severe that it showed through to discolor my skin. My whole body, in fact, had been covered with red and yellow splotches, the result of my blood's inability to absorb all the alcohol I had been drinking.

I hadn't been able to keep down the lightest food because my bleeding stomach was simply unable to digest anything. I had gone, the doctors solemnly informed me, into severe alcohol seizures, convulsions that twisted and jerked my body; my tongue was lacerated from where I had bitten it. My three-day bout with DT's had been so severe that they professed amazement I had made it through. There had been times, just to keep me alive, that they used bottled oxygen. For a week they had pumped me full of megavitamins, keeping me strapped down while my strength slowly returned. They warned me, their faces drawn and unyielding, that if I continued to drink, no one could be held responsible for what would happen to me except myself.

How I wept to hear those words, how I wanted to beg their forgiveness, the forgiveness of everyone—as if somehow their attitude might make a difference to me, as if the "inconvenience" I had caused could be set right with a few words. If there had been a stack of Bibles available; I would have sworn on them: never would I take another drop, never would I lie or cheat or steal to get myself high, never would I be anything but the most upright, clean-living, hard-working father and husband.

I suppose at the moment I really meant everything I said to the doctors, to Darlene, and to myself. I probably thought that I had gone as far as any man could go and still come back. Now that I returned, nothing could induce me to make the trip again. I would never let another drop of alcohol pass my lips, I ferverently swore in response to the equally heartfelt promise Darlene made one afternoon before my discharge. Quite calmly and purposefully she told me that if I were to start up again she would leave me, file for divorce, and fight for every last bit of property. I was shocked then at the seriousness of her tone, frightened at the prospect of being left to my own devices, and more determined than ever to stay dry.

That determination lasted all of an hour. That was how long it took me to find an excuse to steal some of the household money and make a run to the corner store. By the time Darlene returned home from work on my first day out of the hospital, I was lying passed out on the living-room floor. True to her word, she silently packed and was walking out the door just as I lurched back into consciousness. Seeing the suitcases and the sweet face of my daughter as she held her mother's hands and watched me with wisdom far beyond her years, I pleaded, spilling still more tears. I would never touch—but the words turned to stone in my mouth. I couldn't believe them anymore myself. Yet I was equally unable to believe that my family was walking out on me. I cried for a long hour, my fists beating on the door they had walked through, sobbing an ocean of tears, living a lifetime of regrets, making an eternity of promises, until, cried out, my eyes returned to the bottles waiting for me on the living-room floor.

I was alone, sitting out the days, mumbling and figuring, like a miser's hoard, the coinage of my downfall. My fortune was in my misery: my life, at 25, was over. Failure and choking self-pity passed the time with me, ugly but comforting companions. And I had my bottles, so many bottles. When I thought of Darlene and Jerri I wept, and weeping I would drink and in drinking still more haunted images floated up before me. I would weep and I would drink, and then I would pass out. I would wake up alone hours later, in the early morning, a cigarette gone out in my hands, the TV's blanched picture hissing at me, and I'd start all over again.

There was a knock at the door, sounding like a gunshot in the echoing house. I tried to get up, but couldn't rise from the sofa's thick cushions. Another knock, and I tried again. Getting unsteadily to my feet, I swayed back and forth, regarding the door through one eye. I fumbled for one of the cigarettes lying on the coffee table, and waited for another knock. Instead, the doorknob turned and Darlene stepped in, bringing the cool evening air in with her.

"I've got the papers, Gary," she said in a flat voice, without looking at me.

"Darlene," I cried happily, "Darlene honey, I—"

"I've got the papers," she repeated. And she stepped out of the doorway.

"Honey, just come back and let me—" my words tapered off into muttering as a burly sheriff's officer stepped into the room.

"Are you," he glanced at the papers in his hand, "Mr. Gary Bell?"

"He's the one," said Darlene, taking a seat and nodding in my direction. Bitterness and determination formed a mask on her face. She wouldn't look at me; instead, her eyes darted around the room as if searching for damaged goods.

"I'm afraid you'll have to vacate these premises," said the deputy stiffly. "I'm here to serve a legal divorce notice to you, Mr. Bell." He took a step forward. I took one back.

"Get out," spat Darlene, "just get out."

"Let's go quietly, Mr. Bell. We don't want trouble here." The deputy held out his hand.

I swore, "What do you mean?" My words slurred together, my tongue falling over itself. "I . . . this is just as much . . . I . . . ."

"Get out," Darlene said with a deadly calm. "I want you out."

A foul name escaped my lips. The deputy moved toward me and I swung wildly in his direction, losing my footing and almost falling over the coffee table. The TV seemed too loud and the room was spinning. I leaned on him suddenly for support and he grabbed me by the forearm.

"No trouble, Mr. Bell," he repeated. I started to struggle, backing off from the front door that he guided me through. His grip on me tightened.

"Take your hands—" with a sudden jerk he pulled me out the door, letting go as the momentum carried me past the threshold and sent me sprawling onto the lawn.

"Darlene!" I wailed, "You can't do this . . . baby. Please, give me some money, 20 bucks. I've got to find a place to . . . ." I looked desperately around and saw the car. That, I thought, was still mine at least. I'd sleep there tonight. To hell with her. I staggered to my feet and launched myself toward the car.

Darlene came running from the house, passing me. She opened the door of the car and quickly pulled out Jerri, my precious Jerri. The look of fright in the child's eyes cut me down from across the yard. I stopped, staring dumbly at my family, huddling together against me. Suddenly, from behind, the deputy snapped me into a hammerlock, applying a throbbing pressure at the back of my neck.

"Don't make me hurt you, buddy," he said softly into my ear. "Let's you and I go someplace and leave them be, huh?" He forced me toward the open door of his car, bearing down on my neck to get me into the back seat.

Alternately swearing and sobbing uncontrollably, I watched as my wife hurried across the open space to the safety of the front door. Without looking back, she clutched Jerri tightly to her and slammed it shut.

"Darlene," I groaned as the deputy's car sped away, "20 bucks . . . ."

Two months later my father "suggested" that I move to a halfway house in downtown Phoenix. I had been staying with him since Darlene threw me out, and he had endured a lot in that time. First, the divorce had come through, and Darlene's words proved to be prophetic. Everything really *was* hers; she had retained ownership of the house, car, savings account, furniture—every last piece of communal property that had survived our marriage. I spent days in a drunken rage, venting my spleen against her, the lawyers, the judges—against fate itself. It all seemed so unjust. Where, I asked my father endlessly, was "my fair share"? It was just one more blow to my self-esteem, one more reason to blot out the world.

And blot it out I did. My drinking became heavier than ever. Only the scene had changed—this time to my father's small apartment. The accusing eyes of Darlene had been replaced by his eyes, and the shame that gnawed at me for my failures as a husband and parent now became the guilt of failing as a son. My dad, a kind and gentle man, was thrown suddenly into a problem he had no understanding of or control over. To him, the way to solve my addiction was simply to stop. Why, he must have thought to himself, if the stuff has ruined Gary's life and taken his family, his future, and his health away, why on earth can't he just stop?

The DT's returned and with them a wild episode in which I called down carloads of police to stop a burglary in progress: the "little people" again, stealing watches and other valuables off my father's dresser. It was only after hurling drunken insults at an officer who suggested I might try psychiatric treatment that my Dad told me he had moved the missing valuables to the glove compartment of his car to keep me from hocking them for booze money.

I could see, even then, how I was undermining even my father's self-respect. The bad checks, the screaming fits, the blunt warnings from the cops, the ceaseless complaints from the neighbors—all were eroding his reputation and good name. It was only a matter of time before he realized, as so many others had, that there was nothing he could do if I wouldn't help myself. As his only child, he had tried to love me and had sought the advice of many professionals, but there was a point when it was less painful to cut me out of his life than to endure my slow destruction.

When I began showing up at his office, one of the older and more prestigious Phoenix brokerage houses, he had no choice. Dirty and wasted, I would loudly demand money, leering at the secretaries and stealing things from their desks. He was in danger of losing his job, but, as with Darlene, I bitterly resented his "abandonment." How could he do this to me? He knew my problems, knew I couldn't fend for myself. He was tossing me aside, like something used up and useless. I thought nothing of letting him know my feelings, getting vindictive pleasure from the look of torment in his eyes. Still, as painful as it was for him, he held firm, making the arrangements and paying some money toward my bread and board at the halfway house.

Despite my condition, there was something about that house that jolted me into an awareness of just how far I had sunk. Maybe it was the anti-septic smell, the rows of utilitarian bunks in the main dormitory, or the shambling derelicts that had become my housemates.

An urgent sense of desperation clung to me. I had to pull myself together; if I couldn't stop drinking, I at least had to somehow try to accommodate this limitless appetite in my life. I had to get motivated; with everything and everyone I had known now gone (taken from me, I told myself bitterly), whatever I grabbed from that moment on would be mine. I was free at last, I told myself. It was the bitterest joke of all. It was then that I put in a call to Joey.

CHAPTER TEN

Las Vegas

Maybe you've been there, coming through the desert and suddenly finding it like some tawdry carnival in the midst of desolation. Maybe you marveled, as I did that first day, at the fantastic neon sculptures, the wide swatch of blazing light that cuts through the center of the desert twilight and the sound—the endless sound of money clinking and jangling and of chips falling, the shouts of the big winners, the moans of the big losers. Maybe you've watched the women in the tight dresses, with makeup that shines against the harsh night, standing in lines along the street, beckoning, calling and staring from behind dead eyes.

Maybe you've been behind the closed doors, watching the cards fall out on green felt, and heard your heart beat as you put down the chips in a pile. Or maybe you've watched the tiny white squares tumble across the board and heard the muttered whispers of those around you, straining to make the right numbers turn up and face the sky. Maybe you've felt the dry air of dawn as you emerged from a night already fading from memory, with lipstick on your collar, a handful of chips in your pocket and a headache somewhere behind your eyes. Maybe you've walked down the street where only a dry wind follows, and somewhere behind you is the tinny rattle of another chance on the rolling wheels of a one-armed bandit. Maybe you've been to Las Vegas.

Much later, after Vegas itself was a memory, I read something that set me to thinking about that incredible place in the Nevada desert. It seemed that in the old days they used to have places called outlaw cities—fortified towns run by good citizens, with schools and and marketplaces and council halls. If you were a bad guy, outside the law and on the run, you could go to one of those "outlaw cities" and find refuge. The posse couldn't lay a hand on you. It was a place provided for by the law, where even criminals could find a sanctuary. Of course, if you were 50 paces from the main gates and the vigilantes caught up with you, well . . . But once inside, you had made it.

Las Vegas is kind of like that, but with one big difference. Instead of the good citizens running a town for the outlaws to go to, the outlaws run a town for the good citizens to go. And like any good outlaw town, there was nothing that couldn't be had by hook, by crook, and for a price. Most of the good citizens who take a vacation to Las Vegas are lucky if they leave with their pants. That's the way outlaws operate. I'm sure it's not written in the charter of the place, but anybody who arrives in Vegas expecting to work the angles usually gets his own angles worked, and pretty thoroughly.

I was no exception, even if I *was* on the inside track. It was a fast way to live and a faster way to die, and that's just what I was looking for.

Joey was true to his word. I'm sure my forced air of nonchalance over the phone at the halfway house didn't fool him at all. It's hard to keep the crack out of your voice when you're asking the crooked noses for a steady job, but if my old friend noticed anything, he didn't let on. "It's about time," his voice seemed to say; "I'm never wrong about these things, even if you did take longer than I expected." The news that I had left my job at the bank and split from Darlene didn't surprise him in the least; neither, for that matter, was he much affected by my windy explanations about needing more action and a break from the stifling domestic boredom I had so recently shed. The edge of desperation in my voice was obvious, and perhaps it was more a case of honor among thieves that compelled him to stick to his word.

I wanted to leave right away, to join him in Vegas (where he had recently relocated) in order to start enjoying my new life, but Joey told me to wait a week until he had a chance to set things up. He would then meet me in Phoenix, and we would discuss details.

If that week was agonizing, if I ever seriously considered what I was getting myself into during those seven days, then I certainly don't remember it. I'm sure I passed the time as I always did, looking for a drink and cursing the heavens for my fate. As far as Joey and what he might require of me, my mind was made up. There was nothing, I assured myself, left to lose. I had lived for so long on the dark side of respectability that it was foolish for me to pretend anymore that I had any real place in society. I was tired of groveling, of making excuses and looking into a sea of injured and frightened faces, accusing even as they forgave.

With Joey, at least, it wouldn't matter. We were birds of a feather, he and I, with nothing to hide from each other.

It was a stupid lie, and I must have known it even as I repeated it to myself on the way to Joey's club for our meeting. I couldn't and didn't tell him that he was about to hire an alcoholic who couldn't hold a steady job for more than a month at a time. If anything I lied even more boldly to him than to the despised establishment that I was turning my back on. No, it was all bluff and banter, glad-handing and backslapping, even as I hoped that he won't notice the trembling in my hand and the dark circles under my eyes.

"It's going to be a real pleasure working with you," I said, smirking as the waitress set down two double whiskies. While I unended mine in two neat gulps, Joey took a discreet sip before setting down the terms of my employment.

"Gary," he said softly, "you ought to know better than that." The years had given him a mincing, precise air, and he had picked up the habit of meticulously and compulsively cleaning his hands with a large monogrammed handkerchief which he kept in his breast pocket. Everything about him sparkled—his manicure, his rings, his smile, his eyes. Impeccably dressed, he looked for all the world like a highly successful young executive well up the rungs of prosperity. The truth of the matter was something Joey didn't keep from himself. Or me. "When you were a cop, who did they watch more than anyone else in the whole state of Arizona?" The question had a supercilious tone that reflected the sudden switch in our relationship: I was his employee, and things were different now.

The truth was that the police paid equal attention to all top-echelon mobsters in the Phoenix
area, but I knew that wasn't the answer Joey was
looking for. "No one but you, pal," I said,
smiling.

"Right," he said, taking out his handkerchief.
"And if the heat was to see you working for me, it
could be very, very bad. Cops don't like their own
kind going to the other side, and Gary, I'll tell you,
I don't need that kind of trouble."

Personally, I doubted if they would care much,
or even notice, but I didn't say anything. I was
beginning to fear that Joey was trying to give me
the brush-off.

"It's a real problem, Gary, I'm sure you can
see," he continued smoothly, while the cloth
ceaselessly caressed his hands.

"Maybe," I began tentatively, ". . . some of
your friends. I could—"

"I'm way ahead of you, pal," Joey interrupted,
signaling to the waitress for another round. He
pulled a card from the inside pocket of his jacket.
"I want you to go up and see Jack," he said to me,
a smile growing on his face. He had been playing
with me all the time; it was his way of letting me
know who was calling the shots now. The casual
kidding of our former days had disappeared. His
rank, his position in the organization, spoke for
him as he reached again into his pocket and pulled
out an enormous wad of money.

"I want you to get yourself a new outfit," he
said, peeling off a half-dozen large bills and
throwing them on the table next to the business
card. He said it like an insult, but I took the money
(more than I had seen in as long as I could
remember) and with it the card. On it I read a

name. "General Manager" it said beneath the name, and then was listed one of the biggest and most prestigious hotels in Las Vegas. "Be there tomorrow afternoon by 2:00," he directed. "He's expecting you." The waitress set down the order, returning the bold smile that Joey bestowed on her.

I was to be a bodyguard, and it suited me just fine. There was something about the name, some quality of force and authority that I had been lacking for too long. Jack, the hotel manager and my new boss, explained to me the day I arrived why I had been chosen. It wasn't because I was the size of a side of beef; I had, in fact, lost a lot of weight in my bouts with the bottle, and I had never been a muscle man to begin with. It was primarily because I *didn't* look like the kind of guy who smashed heads as easily as cantaloupes that I had been selected for the job. Jack wanted plain, ordinary guys, dressed in business suits, who could move through a crowd like a part of it, making quiet suggestions to people who wanted to rip the tuxedos off celebrities performing in the main room of the hotel. He wanted plain, ordinary guys carrying guns who could take care of a situation without causing a riot. For this I would be getting 700 dollars cold cash a week, a deluxe room in the hotel, and a dose of the good life, Vegas style.

It seemed too good to be true. Six other guys and I were assigned to the detail: any of the big performing stars of the period. They would arrive at the airport for an engagement. We would meet them and escort them back to their suite, usually through the casino's back entrance. Most of the time there was nothing to it. On the few occasions when word leaked out and a mob was there to greet us, the excitement and sense of danger made it all the more exhilarating.

It was exhilarating for *us*, that is. More than once I saw celebrities have to battle their way through a chaotic whirlwind of grasping fingers, clutched autograph books, and flailing limbs. It's no joke, I guess, to have a 500 dollar suit torn from your back, or to be bruised and battered by women literally throwing themselves at you, but from where I stood, I could think of a lot worse ways to get hurt.

All the excitement that surrounded such men—the aura of of immediacy, that sense that you were at the center of some tremendous storm of activity—naturally rubbed off on me. Often, when I'd escort them to the casinos and watch them play the tables like everyone else, seemingly oblivious to the stares that greeted their arrival into any room—often I put myself in their position, and it felt good, as if I belonged there. The influence and power were so real that I could almost taste them. These were men who operated in what seemed complete freedom, without answering to anyone, without explaining anything.

For me, the world I now inhabited was a microcosm of that same boundless freedom. I too had been cut completely loose, with more money and time than I knew what to do with. No one was looking over my shoulder, watching every shot glass and casual binge. There were no clocks to punch, no eight-hour shifts, no five-day weeks. In fact, there was no time at all. As anyone who's been to that town in the middle of the desert will testify, it becomes exceedingly difficult, after awhile, to tell day from night, three in the morning from six in the afternoon. Casinos thrive behind double-thick panes of tinted glass; hotel rooms and brothels always feature heavy curtains; and the outside is rarely glimpsed except from the window of a cab or limousine.

There was nothing that I was not allowed, and a thousand and one distractions. Who was the Gary Bell of a scant few months ago? He simply never existed; it was just part of a bad dream from which I had finally awakened. I fit my new identity like I fit into the wardrobe of the three-piece suits I bought at the rate of one a week. Sex became just one more bit of currency to be thrown down on some gaming table in a mad contest with fortune. Women were not just available, they were prepackaged, inviting baubles that demanded attention—a blonde, a brunette, a redhead—my choice. What day of the week was it, and what struck my continually wandering fancy? I went through the prostitutes and call girls on the Strip like others go through salted peanuts, and it meant just about as much to me.

It's a well-established fact that unchecked freedom breeds boredom, and boredom breeds the need for a more-consuming passion. It's the principle of tolerance (one that I was well familiar with), and it applied to everything that I touched or saw. When one woman wasn't enough, I hired two, and when two began to flag, they'd always have a friend they could call. I could pick them like products off a grocery shelf, naming my pleasure like I named exotic drinks for the bartender to mix. It was sooner than I expected when familiarity bred contempt, and at that moment other, more deadly diversions made themselves known.

CHAPTER ELEVEN

Bruno "The Doctor"

The curtain came down on riotous applause. As the houselights rose on a whistling, stomping audience, we moved from the wings of the stage past chorus girls in brilliant feathered costumes, past dowdy cleaning women, and past stoic, immobile stage hands. "Make way, comin' through," I said, my words muffled against a thick tongue that refused to cooperate. Rounding a corner, I careened into a ladder, and as we rushed past I could hear angry shouts as it crashed to the floor.

I was staggering as I reached the concrete surface of the basement garage, panting to keep up with the others, straining to make out what was in front of me. The car—yes, I could see it and hear the engine purring. Bruno rushed ahead, and I saw his face in the lurid glare of the taillights as he opened the door and waited for the singer to climb in.

We followed him in, two on each side of the singer and one up front with the driver. The long nose of the limo sidled up the ramp and out into the star-streaked night. Immediately the crowd thronged around it, faces pressed against the glass, pushed against the hood, pounding on the roof. The singer looked at me and I could feel the sweat begin to mushroom under my arms. The horn blew, a sound like broken glass in my ears.

Bruno swore. "Step on it," he said to the driver, and then to no one in particular, "Who let the cat out of the bag?" I could barely hear him. I wanted the noise to stop; I needed to get back to the hotel for a good stiff belt, but the car had stopped dead in a swamp of people. The singer looked frightened and Bruno had to shout to be heard. "We've gotta clear it," he said. Suddenly, from either side of me, the doors opened and I was out in the crowd, maddened now by the sight of the opened doors and the sudden possibility of access.

"Shut it!" I heard Bruno scream into my ear, and by simple reflex I swung the door closed, catching someone's hand with the sound of crunching bone. An agonized shriek was lost amidst the pounding and chanting of the singer's name while I tried to follow Bruno and Frank up the front of the car to try and clear some of the people off the hood. Before I could take a step, I stumbled, fell against the fender, and slid onto the pavement. Feet trampled me, pushing my chest into the asphalt, still warm from the blazing sun of the day. A heel flattened onto my knuckles and hot pain coursed up my arm. It was only as blackness began to surround me and I was falling headlong into unconsciousness that I felt a strong arm life me off the street and into the tense, silent car, pushing away into the night, gathering speed to leave the frenzied throng behind.

"You're gonna blow this gig, Bell, and I'm not gonna cover for you forever." Bruno took a savage belt of his drink, throwing back his head, gasping against the burning liquor and regarding me with a baleful eye. It was quiet now, some early-morning hour when only the hardest cases—the old women and strange men in trench coasts and ragged trousers—worked the slots, oblivious to all but the sight of bells, plums, and cherries. The trembling had subsided; the experience of earlier that evening had faded into an alcoholic haze as I listened with half an ear to what he was saying. All I really knew about what had happened was an ache in my hand, bruised by a spike heel. I had been working hard to forget the rest—the sudden terror, the pain and nausea, and the chagrin at muffing my duties so utterly. The shame was gone, and the pain would subside with another drink or two, but still Bruno kept buzzing in my ear.

"Look," he said, "it's no business to me what you do in your off time, but it's really starting to show on the job. You coulda gotten us all into a lot of trouble, Bell, and by rights I should tell Jack about it." I regarded him with bleary and uncomprehending eyes. I knew he was telling me something important, but all I could think about was the redhead down the bar who was checking me out with all the subtlety of a butcher eyeing a side of beef.

"You're not even listening, are you?" Bruno said, with a gesture of disgust that momentarily startled me from my daze. "Listen, I don't owe you a thing, Bell. I don't even like you very much, but even a sucker like you deserves a break." He reached into his coat pocket and pulled out a bottle of pills. Opening it, he laid three small white specimens on the bar. I looked at them, trying to count, trying to fix them in my swimming field of vision. "We've got a pickup at the airport at 4:00 this afternoon," he continued disdainfully. "Go to sleep and put in a call for 2:30. When you get up take these. Maybe then you'll pull your own weight."

I got unsteadily to my feet, winking at the redhead and holding up my room key. Bruno was right—I needed some sack time. I took two steps before I felt his hand on my arm. "Hey, genius," he said, trying without success to keep the amusement from his voice, "You forgot your pills."

Bruno was the closest thing I had to a friend in those early days in Vegas. He was "The Doctor," a tall, lanky Ivy Leaguer from a respectable Boston family who, in some other lifetime, had actually gone to medical school. His wry wit and easy, familiar manner made him popular among the hotel's patrons and employees, and he was widely known as one of the town's more flamboyant spenders. He was the kind of guy who attracted others to him, a natural function of his height and worldly air. And I guess compared with most of the mugs we worked with he was a guy with brains and class, and the fact was that by the prevailing standards of our world, they were right. Most people can sense breeding, particularly in a fleshpot like Vegas, where most of the clientele have nothing more to offer than simple avarice and greed. Bruno, who had picked up his nickname of "Doctor" long before I ever made his acquaintance, was the kind of guy who made sure the carnation in his lapel was always fresh, that the woman on his arm was there because she wanted to be (not because she had been bought and paid for), and that no one ever, for one moment, took him for granted.

He was also a textbook-perfect case of a compulsive criminal. He was a man with all the breaks—from a privileged class, well-educated, good-looking, and exuding charm. But Bruno had one overriding passion that all else was subjugated to—the need to break the law. Don't ask me why—why, after having it all, he threw it all away. Perhaps he knew something the rest of us didn't. Perhaps he saw that lawlessness extends far beyond class and social barriers, the rip-offs and scams are as much a part of corporate politics as the back-alley life of a common hood. Maybe he knew it from the top: those pimps and prostitutes that ply their trade in mansions behind manicured lawns and well-tended rose gardens, who count their take in tens of thousands instead of tens and twenties. Maybe he knew that for every con man serving time on some petty rap there was a bigger fish swimming free, getting fat and glossy behind a facade of respectability. Maybe, finally, he knew what respectability really was—just another system, another game where the odds were in your favor not because you deserved it but because you were born to it.

But we never talked about this. We didn't have to; it was understood. He was a man who loved risk and danger, who accepted them as part of the turf. The only thing he never really came to terms with was the wasted potential of his own life—what he had thrown away, and the bitter price of what replaced it.

His surgeon's background wasn't the only reason he was known in some circles as "The Doctor." That name had a far more practical origin: Bruno knew about drugs—where to get them, what they did, the best combinations, and the fastest way to get there—than anyone else in town. He was the supplier of the purest drugs, the teacher of the novice, the sage that cured what ailed you. But in my case what cured me almost killed me.

Bruno knew that I wasn't going to hang onto my job for long if I kept drinking at the rate I was going. That night outside the hotel, when the mob very nearly killed me because I could hardly see to stand, he had proven the point to his satisfaction. It was from that point on that he undertook my "education."

For Bruno drugs were a sublime manifestation of control, the control which our own bodies so often deny us. Drugs can obliterate the symptoms of physical problems, destroy the need for sleep, dispel depression, and sharpen the senses to a razor edge. Every subtle combination yields certain benefits to a razor edge. Every subtle combination yields certain benefits for the knowledgeable user—a pinch here, a taste there, fine-tuning a high to exact specifications to meet any whim and every contingency.

Bruno knew all the drugs by their medical names, and there wasn't an hour of the day or night when he couldn't get for you the very combination your heart desired. A walking pharmacy, he dispensed powders and pills like a gypsy fortune-teller dispenses lies, suiting the customer to the treatment. For him it wasn't a way to make a living; the popular image of the monstrous dope-pusher who gives out a little to hook his clients was altogether too crude for Bruno. I really think it gave him pleasure—a warped and evil pleasure, to be sure, but a real satisfaction nonetheless. We would come to him as children and he would take us to heaven for a few hours. After that, if the edge got a little blunted, and the euphoria turned to a lingering unease, and the warm glow faded, well, The Doctor always had that little extra something to put out the lights. And when you woke up, there was another party-colored pill to give the morning a boost.

Amphetamine, Methedrine, cocaine, Seconal, phenobarbital, opium, heroin, morphine—it always amazed me later that I hadn't entered the shadow world inhabited by these names earlier in my obsessive career. Booze, of course, remained my strictest and most exacting taskmaster, but what a variety of sensations, of warm rushes and tingling excitement, I had overlooked! No longer did I have to worry about stumbling around out of control like the alcoholic I was. No need for that. An upper, a downer, a little chemical modulation, and I was Joe Normal. No one knew but me; no one could point to me and shake his head in disapproval. Thanks to The Doctor, I had control over myself once again. I could adjust my state to suit myself, and if I needed to break up an unruly mob to get a singer to the airport in time—no problem. There was a galaxy of pills at my disposal, a desert of powders, an ocean of solutions.

I took to each new experience like a kid at a toyshop clearance. From speed I graduated quickly to heroin. The fact that the first few times that I injected the deadly drug into the muscles of my forearm ("skin popping") made me violently ill had absolutely no effect on my pursuit of the high. From muscle injections I went directly to mainlining. The resultant express-train rush up my veins to the control centers of my brain gave me an instant lesson in this ancient and most insidious form of addiction. I can only look to the sky in silent thanks that this horrifying powder refined from the opium poppy did not exert its spell over me. I tried, believe me I tried—I *wanted* to get hooked on heroin. After all, most of the guys I worked with were strung out on the stuff, and I rarely saw a prostitute in the cold light of day that didn't show the telltale hollow eyes and trail of destruction up the veins of both arms. If it was good enough for them . . . the old rationale, but I just couldn't get into the swing.

Instead, I took to uppers, meth and dexys, powders and pills, alone and in combination. The illusory sense of heightened awareness, the bounce in my step and the glint in my eyes, gave me a world-conquering sense of superiority that I reveled in. I learned quickly to relish the glow that spread up from my abdomen ten minutes after swallowing two, three, four, or more innocuous-looking white pills. I loved equally the instant acceleration I experienced after snorting a few lines of pure crystal meth. My head would snap to attention, my heels would almost click, I would straighten my tie and slick back my hair, and I would head out into the night looking for the action that would suit my sense of complete ascendancy. "Sitting on top of the world" doesn't even come close to explaining my sense of self-esteem in those moments; I was a god walking the earth, capable of leveling with a glance, commanding obedience with a gesture, turning all to suit my pleasure with nothing more than thought.

But that was nothing in comparison to the thrill I soon discovered by mixing speed with my old companion, alcohol. It was like being high forever; I'd pop a handful of my little white helpers and I could literally drink all night long without ever stopping or ever getting to the sloppy point, the place of diminishing returns where your feet refuse to cooperate and the floor has a nasty habit of rushing up and hitting you in the face. Speed and booze soon became my exclusive diet, and things never looked better. Of course, there was a toll, a real and measurable toll, but if I had known about it (it wasn't something The Doctor explained when he handed out the goodies) it wouldn't have made a bit of difference. Even if I had been able to feel the millions of brain cells dissolving with each snort and every pill, even if I could have measured the strain on my heart as it raced to the demonic tune of the drugs coursing through my veins, even if I could have seen the way the alcohol ate away at the lining of my stomach or tore at the fibers of my liver, I'm sure I would have looked somewhere else—to the next bar with a good-looking whore.

CHAPTER TWELVE

The Collectors

I hadn't been working for Jack more than three months—staying high, serving myself, and living a life that grew more and more unreal with each passing day—when I was called to the office of the hotel manager for a "job evaluation." Jack, a short, dark man with a brusque and businesslike air, was waiting in his penthouse suite with Joey, looking as coolly relaxed and detached as ever. I was more than a little nervous at seeing my old friend; regardless of how willing I had been to do my job, take orders, and ask no questions, there always hovered the distinct possibility that somehow, someday, I might cross the fine line between propriety and presumption that existed in the organization that Joey was part of.

That would be the day, I had no doubt, when some guys in shiny suits would come knocking on my door and take me for a ride. Had Joey heard a bad report about my drinking? Had Bruno or the singer reported my ineptness the night of the near-riot? Or had I broken some other rule, one I didn't even know about? My sweating palms attested to a lot more than the double dose of speed I had downed before arriving for the meeting.

"Joey tells me you used to be in collections," Jack said by the way of introduction. The soaked nub of a cigar rolled between his lips to make way for the words. That's it, I thought to myself—they had found out about the whole sordid mess: the drinking, the DT's, losing my job and my family. There was no use denying it. I nodded mutely.

"In a bank," Jack continued, rising from behind his desk and walking over to the spacious window overlooking the desert flatlands.

"Like I told you, Jack," said Joey, winking at me. "It's perfect for him. Right, Gary?" I began to feel more at ease. Joey was playing with me again. He knew perfectly well what was going on in my mind and was in no hurry to set me at ease. but at least, I told myself, he wasn't measuring me for cement galoshes. I even managed a smile and a measure of my old bantering self-confidence. "If you say so, Joey, then it must be true."

He laughed and turned to Jack, still looking out the window as twilight settled over the limitless expanse. "We got a bank here too, Gary," Jack said softly; "people make deposits in it all night long." It was his turn to laugh as he faced us, stepping over to the intercom on his desk. "Margie," he said, switching it on. "Can you bring in that information now?" "Right away," answered a tinny voice, and a moment later his secretary laid a sheet of paper on the desk. We all watched silently as she swayed from the room. It was Joey who broke the silence with a low, appreciative whistle.

"We got collection problems in our bank too," Jack said, perusing the piece of paper. "Same kind of thing I'm sure you ran into. You know, deadbeats, smart guys, con men.''

I nodded, remembering the sordid grind back in Phoenix.

''So what we figured was this. Maybe you could help us with our problems, seeing as you're an expert. At least that's what Joey tells me. Would you call yourself an expert, Gary?'' He paused, relighting what remained of his cigar with the gaudy gold lighter on his desk top. I wasn't sure exactly what he was getting at, but I instinctively tried to hold onto what I already had: a comfortable, well-paying gig.

''I really like bodyguard work,'' I said, ''The guys and I get along real well . . . .''

'' I think you'll enjoy this job a lot more,'' Joey interjected. ''In fact, I know you will. It's a lot more . . . creative.'' Out came the handkerchief as he began the careful ritual of cleaning his hands.

''You'll be working with the same boys you are now,'' offered Jack, ''and there'll be a little something extra in it for you.'' He reached down to open the desk drawer, pulling out an envelope and handing it to me. I quickly counted 12 hundred-dollar bills inside.

''Congratulations,'' said Joey, ''you've just been promoted.'' The phone rang and Jack answered it. I sensed that the interview was at an end. Turning to leave, I walked a few steps toward the door before I heard my name.

''Hey,'' Jack called, his hand over the receiver, ''where you going?''

''You guys look busy,'' I said. ''I thought I'd do a little celebrating.'' My heart was fluttering, perhaps from relief or perhaps from some sense of premonition.

"No time for that," Jack said. He picked up a sheet of paper from his desk and held it out to me. "You and Bruno have some work to do. You better get on it."

Taking the sheet, I saw a name and address typed in the exact center. It was a fashionable suburb in Orange County, below Los Angeles. Next to it was the figure $14,670. The last thing I noticed as I left the room was Joey's sardonic smile.

The neighborhood was quiet and spacious, with wide streets and sweeping lawns. An occasional station wagon rolled by, carrying a housewife to her morning shopping. It was a typical Southern California morning, full of the promise of a brilliantly sunny day. We pulled to the curb in a rented car and sat for a moment, looking at the comfortable ranch-style home with the hedges trimmed and the windows revealing a glimpse of the brick fireplace. Beyond, in the breakfast room, was a man sitting with the morning paper, drinking a cup of coffee and talking to a woman with her hair in curlers. It wasn't yet 8:30. On another day he would soon be leaving for work. Today it was going to be different.

"Here," said Bruno as he pulled a small vial of white powder from his coat pocket. He tapped out a heap of crystal Methedrine on the back of his hand, and with a quick motion inhaled it. Almost immediately the clean, exhilarating rush coursed up from my stomach, spreading through my arms and legs, putting hum in my ears and a slight dryness in my mouth. I was ready! "Follow my lead," The Doctor continued. "Don't go too far. This is the first; there'll be others." He opened the car door, and the smell of new-mown grass wafted in.

I pushed the bell, looking down for a moment at the rubber mat that offered WELCOME as the muted chimes rang inside. A quiet moment passed as my pulse beat fast and steady. The door opened and a middle-aged woman in a housecoat answered, smiling. "Can I help you?" she asked, and in that instant I absorbed everything about her. Her face, without makeup at this early hour, reflected a fading but still-radiant beauty. She trusted life, and why not? She had been provided with the amenities that make living a comfortable, pleasing passage. Civic duties, the PTA, some social cause or another—these were the idle pastimes that occupied her. If she had been lied to, she didn't know it. If she suspected what her husband did on those long business weekends, she either didn't care or didn't show it. A placid and well-bred smile showed complete confidence in the world she had created for herself by marriage, by station and by a carefully groomed self-image.

"Is this the home of—" Bruno glanced down at the slip of paper in his hand—"Lawrence Delwell?" She nodded, still smiling, looking into both our faces as from the kitchen we heard his voice call, "Who is it, honey?"

Bruno smiled back. "Listen, honey, why don't you tell Larry we want to talk to him?" he winked.

The smile on her face froze. As I watched, my blood raced. It was a totally unexpected thrill to see this woman, this stranger, feel fear flickering in the corners of her mind.

"Do you know my husband?" she asked icily.

"Tell him to come to the door, lady," I said, my voice soft and utterly devoid of emphasis. It had a chilling effect on her, and I felt like laughing out loud at her vulnerability, her ignorance at what was coming. Her smile had vanished; her mouth was a tight line, eyes darting between us and beyond, past the front lawn to the street, as if she expected to find an answer there.

"Is there something wrong?" she asked, and in her voice I could hear the sinking sensation. "Is there—"

"Get Larry, Mrs. Delwell," repeated Bruno, and at that moment Larry emerged from around the door, smiling as his wife had smiled before him, putting his hand on her shoulder and saying, "What is it, honey? I think the eggs are burning."

His eyes met mine. Nothing. No recognition of what was going to happen. He was a little overweight and his face was pink, scrubbed, and shaven. His tie cut into the beginning of a double chin, and the touch of gray at his temples was surely something he was proud of. He was a businessman, a successful businessman with some bad habits. "Can I help you, gentlemen?" he asked brightly.

"Larry—" his wife began, but was cut short by Bruno.

"You Lawrence Delwell?" he said, his tone turned from bantering to deadly serious. The man nodded.

"We've got a little matter of 15,000 dollars, Mr. Delwell. I think you know what I'm talking about." A slice of silence followed, and we all watched—Bruno, the woman, and I—as the man's face turned ashen.

"I . . . I . . . explained to your Mrs. . . . Mrs. . . . um, the woman at your office, that I would, um be sending—" he gulped, the lump struggling to get past the knot in his tie. Sweat had suddenly sprung up on his forehead, and when Bruno cut him short

I watched him flinch. I could barely contain what was going on inside me. Anticipation raced along the path which the drug had etched in my brain, burning my nerves and putting a fine mist of sweat on my forehead and the palms of my hands.

"We don't know anything about that," said Bruno, sucking his teeth. "We're here to collect 15,000 dollars."

"Larry," his wife said, her voice trembling, "who are these men? What do they want? What 15,000 dollars? Larry—"

"A little gambling debt, Mrs. Delwell," I said, with the same deadly calm. "Maybe we should step inside . . ."

"Gambling?" she repeated, her voice rising. "What are you talking about? My husband doesn't gamble. Larry, tell them you don't know what they're talking about. You must have the wrong house . . ."

"We've got the right house, lady," I said, and the look of panic on the man's face sent a shiver up my spine. "Why don't you let us in?"

"I most certainly will not, I've never—" she began, and I saw her husband's hand tighten on her shoulder.

"Look," he said, "I told your people—"

"I don't care what you told our people, Larry," said Bruno, mocking the blustering tone of the man. "We want 15,000 dollars."

"If you don't leave this property right away, I'm going to call—" the woman shouted, and suddenly, in a frozen second, I saw Bruno's hand shoot out and shove her back through the doorway, sending her sprawling across the parquet floor.

"Hey!" shouted the man, moving with sudden speed toward Bruno, only to be stopped by the muzzle of a .38 in his stomach. A low groan escaped from somewhere deep inside him.

"Larry," sobbed his wife from the foyer. "Larry, what do they want? Tell them it's not you, Larry . . ."

"Yeah, tell us, Larry," I said pushing past him and into the house. A burning smell was coming from the kitchen. "You better get those eggs, Mrs. Delwell," I said, pulling the gun from its cradle under my arm. "Don't try and use the phone, all right? Larry wants everything to go smoothly, right, pal?" and I turned to him, smiling.

"Do what he says," the man told his wife, and pleaded, "Listen, I don't have 15,000 dollars. I just don't have it right now. My daughter just started college—"

"You should have thought of that at the crap table, Larry," Bruno said mildly as he pulled the gun from the man's spreading midriff. "I suggest you figure out a way to get it. Real quick."

The woman, still sobbing, got off the floor and went down the hall to the kitchen. I watched her retreat, gazing at her figure beneath the thin housecoat.

"I'm telling you, I don't have—" the man's words went spinning off into the air as he reeled backwards, blood splattering from his mouth. Bruno stood, the butt of his .38 flecked with blood, his arm descending from the quick upward arc that had brought the steel grip across the man's face, dislodging teeth, tearing his lower lip, and sending a wet smacking sound reverberating down the hall. The woman shrieked at the sight of her husband bent over, with blood dripping on the shiny floor. Her eyes flashed to the gun in my hand. Her mouth was still open, although no sound escaped, as she turned and bolted down the corridor.

A few quick strides and I had caught up with her. Grabbing her by the hair, I jerked hard and threw her into a straight-backed chair that stood beneath a coat rack. Wordlessly I pointed the gun at her temple, putting a forefinger across my lips and shaking my head. Not a word, my gesture said, not a sound.

"Don't hurt her," the man said, from what seemed a long way off down the hall. His voice almost drowned in the liquid that filled his mouth. "Leave her alone. I'll get the money. I'll get it . . ."

"We'll wait," said Bruno as smoke from the burning eggs began to drift out of the kitchen. "Maybe the little lady'll cook us up some breakfast."

It was early afternoon before the phone rang. Bruno was watching a soap opera on televison while I sipped bourbon from the man's liquor chest, sitting with the gun in my hand, watching the woman. She stared dully out the plate-glass window overlooking the Japanese garden that was their backyard. Hummingbirds hovered around the honeysuckle vines that crept up the walls. The sun was casting shadows across the willow tree and over the still fishpond.

On the coffee table in front of us were the remains of our long wait—breakfast dishes smeared with egg yolks and sprinkled with bread-crumbs; the morning paper, its crossword puzzle half-done; empty beer cans spilling out on the carpet; and Bruno's vial, its white powder nearly gone. The pool of blood by the front door slowly coagulated in the air-conditioned room.

"I've got it," said the man over the phone. His voice sounded far away, strained, and indistinct.

"Is it cash?" I asked, nodding to Bruno and the woman, who had started at the sound of the phone and now trembled as her eyes questioned me.

"Let me speak to my wife," he said, and I imagined his mouth, broken and swollen trying to form the words. What had they thought happened to him at the bank, or the loan office, or wherever he went to raise the money? I thought to myself. Maybe he said he cut himself shaving. I almost laughed.

"How much did you get?" I asked, ignoring his plea.

"The whole thing," he said, "in cash. Let me speak to my wife."

I caught Bruno's eye. He gestured for the phone, so I rose and brought it over to him. Cradling the receiver in the crook of his neck, he lit a cigarette, waited a long moment, and said, "Larry, I want to make sure everything's going smoothly. Did you get the whole thing?" The only sound in the house was the drone of the television set as Bruno nodded and smiled across to the woman. "Good, good, yes, very good, Larry. Yes, yes, she's right here. And as soon as you bring us the 20,000 dollars we'll be on our way like nothing happened." Another long silence, punctuated by the tinny voice of the man shouting on the other end. Bruno held the receiver away from his ear, grimacing. I laughed and took another pull on the bourbon bottle.

Flicking his ash on the floor, Bruno said to the man, "No, no . . . Larry . . . Larry, listen to me. Twenty grand, pal. It's a service charge. You better hurry, Lar, the banks close—" he glanced at his watch— "in about an hour." He gently replaced the receiver back on the phone, winked at the woman, and returned to the television.

It was nearly twilight when the man returned with a briefcase. Opening the door with his key, he entered the hallway, stepped across the dried patch of his own blood, and cautiously moved into the living room.

"We're in here, Larry," said Bruno, rousing me from a half-sleep. "Welcome home."

With a cry, the woman rose from the sofa and rushed to her husband. She tried to kiss him, but he drew back with a wince of pain, his mouth purple and distorted, a broken front tooth visible behind the lacerated lip.

"I couldn't, " he mumbled in pain; "I couldn't get the other 5,000 dollars. Please, I paid off the debt. Leave us alone." He held out the briefcase, the woman clinging to him and moaning, "Please," he repeated.

"Listen, Larry," said Bruno, getting up and taking the case, "we don't work for nothing. I suggest you make some calls and get the rest of the bread."

"I can't," he said' "I've been . . . to everyone . . . I just—" and he began to sob along with his wife. With a disgusted look, Bruno turned to me. I got up too, tipping over the coffee table in the process. A corner of the table cracked into the television picture tube, and with a crackle and pop of electricity the screen shattered.

"Let's go, buddy, Let's find that money," I said, and pried hs wife away. The woman could no longer speak; her moans had turned to strangled, broken sounds as she watched us take her husband, one on each side, out the front door and into the cool evening air.

"Please," was all he could say, tears coursing down his face, pulling and jerking at our grip without strength. "Please."

When we reached the curb he stumbled and fell, halfway into the gutter. He lay on his face, his body trembling violently, unable to get up. I watched him for a long moment, while Bruno shook his head in disgust.

"You make me sick," I said, and then, slowly and deliberately, taking careful aim, I raised my foot and brought it down with sudden and vicious force across his forearm where it lay over the curb. The sound of splintering bone still echoes in my ear.

CHAPTER THIRTEEN

The Phoenix Plan

I worked my "collecting" job as long as I could, traveling around with slips of paper in my pocket and a gun beneath my armpit, thirsting for vengeance. The pattern was soon set: whatever the amount we were sent out to collect we would add a "service charge," usually around two grand, and split the take. The bad risks, as I said, came from all walks of life—lawyers, doctors, con men, and hard losers. To say that I didn't get to enjoy the terror I inflicted on others would be lying—I got to the point of hoping they wouldn't have the money so I could put a hurt on them.

The drugs and booze helped to make the work go smoothly. My intake of speed was rapidly approaching that of the alcohol, and the tolerances I was achieving amazed even Bruno. It's not that he tried to slow me down—that wasn't in the book of etiquette. He just watched, smiled his enigmatic smile and waited.

He didn't have to wait long. The fall, that awful, sickening plunge, came not more than 18 months after I had moved from Phoenix to Las Vegas. It was the hospital again—the screaming fits, the little people under the bed, and the hideous agony in my gut. Then, like dawn after the blackest night, there was a slow coming together, with regular meals, plenty of sleep, and a chance to let my ravaged body restore itself as best it could. At last I was on my feet again, standing in the full light of day, wearing an expensive suit and a nice pair of shoes, but without a penny to my name and nowhere to go.

Jack and Joey were, of course, out of the question. It had been made clear to me, without a lot of excess explaining, that while they didn't care what I did in my off hours, certain things were expected of me. In that respect, beating up people for bad gambling debts was just another job I couldn't hold down, like being a cop or working in a bank. I never bothered to go back to the hotel, to look up the old gang and get back into the swing of things. It wouldn't have washed.

So I went back to Phoenix, to my dad, to the halfway house and the old masquerade of drinking while pretending not to. One of the requirements for residence at the halfway house (my dad, by this time, was too wise to let me back into his apartment) was that I had to look for a job. It was easy enough to scrounge some money off the old man, spend the day in some dive, and return in the evening with a tale of woe about the scarcity of an honest day's work.

I imagine the cycle would have repeated indefinitely if I hadn't gotten a call one evening on the pay phone in the hallway of the halfway home.

"Gary, that you?" I recognized Bruno's voice immediately and was at that moment very glad indeed to hear from him. I had, after all, taken quite a fall from my former free-wheeling status in Jack's employ, and Bruno represented a link to a past that I sorely missed just about then.

"Bruno, you son-of-a-gun, where are you?"

"I'm in town," was his reply, and I could almost see the sardonic glint in his eye. "I had a hell of a time tracking you down."

"How did you find me?" I asked excitedly. "Are you down here on a job?"

"Job? No, haven't you heard?" he replied, "I quit. About the same time you did."

I laughed, and Bruno joined me. It wasn't just like old times. "Hey," I said lowering my voice. "How about meeting me downtown for a drink? I could be there in 20 minutes."

"You took the words right out of my mouth, pal," said The Doctor; "just name the place."

He was waiting for me in a booth, surrounded by three men I had never seen before. As I sidled in, ordering a double, Bruno began the introductions.

"Gary," he said, "I'd like you to meet a couple of old friends of mine from back East. Eddie—" a short, swarthy man with a nervous smile offered his hand. It was clammy. "Frank—" at least as tall as Bruno, with a lantern jaw and huge, ungainly hands. "And Chester—" he grunted, tipped back his clean-shaven head to swallow his Scotch, and regarded me coolly. Bruno continued, "I'd like you to meet Gary."

"A pleasure," I said, thinking more about the drink that was on its way than the decidely unsavory bunch crowded in the booth. If I was still a cop, I thought to myself, this is one group I'd run in for questioning.

Bruno and I caught up on each other for a few minutes. I carefully avoided revealing the real cause of my sudden disappearance from work, but I knew even as I fabricated some nonsense about coming down with a "bad bug" that The Doctor knew the real story. Nevertheless, he nodded sagely and shook his head in sympathy. After my second drink had arrived, while I was regaling him with the fictional job prospects I had lined up in Phoenix, the one called Chester suddenly leaned over and whispered into Bruno's ear. Still nodding and smiling, Bruno muttered something under his breath to the bald man and turned to me.

"Chester thinks it's time we get down to business," he said.

"Business?" I said, "What business?"

"You know that big discount store on the east end of town? The one in the shopping complex?" Bruno asked blithely.

I nodded.

"That's business." he said. "Tomorrow night." And, raising his glass, he offered a toast. "To partners."

CHAPTER FOURTEEN

Holdup!

Somewhere a church bell chimed: seven . . . eight . . . nine . . . ten. I looked out the side of the window at the half-emptied parking lot. Women pushed their shopping carts across the neon-lit distance; children laughed or cried, their voices barely audible through the tinted glass of the stolen car. Beyond, out to the boulevard, horns sounded and a jet passed overhead in the smothering Southwestern darkness. Further out, unheard, a coyote howled against the rising moon, and dry wind rose across the unbroken expanse, gusting away from bright lights.

As the muffled chimes faded, I looked down to my watch; it was 30 seconds slow. I looked across to Eddie; as our eyes connected, he nodded. Shutting off the engine, I turned to the back seat. "Ready?" Nods. I sat for a moment, very still, feeling my heart and my pulses beating steadily against the weight of the .357. I was very calm, very high. I had reached exactly the right pitch; my nerves were tingling and my brain was functioning with crystalline logic. I had total motor control, totally tuned senses, I moved effortlessly as I opened the door and stepped out into the hot night.

Behind me I heard the others getting out too, and together we walked toward the towering glass facade of the store. Looming up before us, the rows of double doors swung open and closed as we came nearer, gliding smoothly in towards our target. Chicano families hovered near the entrance, waiting for cars to gather their packages while children clung to their mothers' dresses or rode painted animals for a dime, up and down.

Without rushing or weaving, I moved straight ahead, feeling the others on either side of me, past the news racks and onto the rubber mats painted with scuffed arrows pointing in. We stopped. With a hiss, the door in front of us opened, and we made for the shining steel turnstyles, moving down the center aisle.

We passed rows of cheap leisure suits, baby mannequins in sleepers, a "Back To School" banner, and trays of plaids and solids. Shirts, a pyramid-stack of tennis-ball canisters, dummies in hiking boots, and camping gear gave way to more and yet more merchandise.

Even as I walked I was aware of how I must have looked, my normality hiding the intent from casual glances. I could feel my clothes moving on me as I walked, the holster tugging at my shoulder with the weight of the piece. No one paid attention as the others peeled off and Bruno and I made our way to the rear of the store. We were just two more customers looking for a bargain. We walked diagonally through Garden Aids, Toys, Greeting Cards, and Paperbacks towards the small office to our left. My eyes saw everything, my ears caught every sound—the cough in the next aisle, the demonstration TV's to the right, the reedy violins playing country-and-Western tunes over the PA.

I was in complete control of every factor—not just my eyes and feet, bringing me inexorably to the corner of the store; not just the speed coursing through my blood and singing in my skull; not just the gun, the shells, the trigger, the weapon that brought with it the elation of power; not any of these more than the cold confidence that very soon I would act. A slight shudder of anticipation traced up my spine.

Turning a corner of the last aisle, around stacks of mops and brooms, I stopped, looking again at my watch. Fifty-five . . . fifty-eight; good. A minute—perfect. Bruno caught my eye. Reaching into his coat pocket, he pulled out a length of stocking. I did the same, facing him and pulling the sheer sheath over my head. Opening my eyes inside the nylon, I saw a middle-aged woman behind the window of the credit office, her fingers flying over the keys of her adding machine. Vision defined now by the tiny mesh of the material, I looked back to Bruno and nodded.

It was time. Quickly we moved off, Bruno grabbing a shopping bag off the shelf and folding it under his arm. I could hear our steps as we gathered speed, taking aim at the frosted window of the office door.

As it swung open the middle-aged woman looked up, her face draining of color, changing as it assumed the contours of sudden fear, molding to the sense of danger, her eyes reflecting only the will to survive. I could see clearly, through the hose, her face turn a deathly white, only to rush back in a flush as I raised the .357 and pointed it at her head. From two feet away I could smell her perfume and read the numbers on the adding machine and the title of the paperback book lying open on her desk. There were a million details, and I caught them all. The gun, an extension of my hand now, was warm with body heat. From the edge of my vision I saw that two other people were in the small room. Bruno had them both under the barrel of his gun, sitting on the manager's desk as the man peered up through thick glasses, his hands in the air like a Western-movie bank clerk. Behind him a young black woman stood, her face pulled tight. The next thing I heard was the tick of the wall clock, far off across the room, and the sound of my own voice—smooth, well-modulated, reasonable in the moment of tension.

"Do what you're told and you won't get hurt. We're here for one thing. That's all." I looked the woman near to me in the eye. I had read her name plaque, pinned to her blouse, as soon as I had walked into the room. "The combination, Mary Ellen," I said, matching the calm of my voice deliberately centering the sight of my gun at her forehead. Details, details—nothing escaped my notice: the vein pulsing at her temple, her eyes fluttering from me to the hole at the end of the barrel and back, the paralysis of terror catching hold. I could almost taste her fear and experience for myself the desperately fine line between living and dying. Panicked, her eyes broke away, darting to the corner of the desk where the manager sat.

"We're going to open the safe now," Bruno said, gesturing with the gun for the manager to stand. Bruno's grotesque features moved inside the the nylon mask as he spoke.

Glancing at my watch, and still holding the gun at Mary Ellen's head from across her desk, I thought of the others, in position now at the cash registers in front of the store. The shopping bags would already be opened, the black money trays being emptied, the larger bills scooped up from underneath. I could still hear trebly music, muffled through the shut door. Just then I saw a man come around the aisle, looking intently at a list and pushing a cart full of cans of motor oil and a small child. The child looked straight a me, perplexed by my flattened features and the tassel of stocking on top of my head. As the man wheeled around the corner, the child laughed and pointed before being cut from sight behind a display of kitchen aids.

Mary Ellen was looking at me. Her eyes, furtively searching my face, dropping quickly to her hands, frozen on the desk, when I returned her gaze and gestured for her to stand. "We know exactly what we're doing," I said, while the manager crouched over the safe, turning the dial noiselessy left and right. "Lie down on the floor," I told Mary Ellen. "Spread your feet."

"You too," I heard Bruno mutter to the black woman. They both got silently to the floor. The manager, with Bruno standing over him, pulled open the thick door of the safe, revealing its dark interior with the stacks of bills, tagged and wrapped, waiting. I was still pointing the gun at Mary Ellen as I nodded to Bruno, who opened his shopping bag and started passing the stacks into its mouth.

Both women lay perfectly still on the floor. They were so quiet—they hardly breathed, as if already dead instead of only trying with every muscle to look that way, to avoid the attention of my eyes and the terrible hole of the barrel. Quiet. Listening. Praying.

The shopping bag was three-quarters full. The safe was empty except for its ledgers, coins, and legal papers. "With them," Bruno told the manager, who took his place on the floor beside the two women.

"Five minues," I said. "That's all we're asking for. Stay where you are, wait five minutes, and we won't have to come looking for you." I knelt down and put the .357's barrel behind Mary Ellen's right ear. "Understand?"

At the touch of cold metal to her skin, she jerked violently in shock and horror away from the point of steel, and screamed, a strangled breathless sound rending the thick silence of the office. In the next thin segment of that second, reacting to the scream and the quick movement of her head, I pulled the trigger. It was just the slightest, almost imperceptible movement of my forefinger, but I heard it. So did Mary Ellen. Her body sagged, a helpless groan escaping before she sank into unconsciousness. Nothing had happened. Nothing. Suddenly I felt the sweat under my arms, on my forehead, in the palms of my hands, soaking me. Nothing had happened—no explosion, no burning smell of gun powder, no ringing in my ears. Nothing.

Bruno made his way around the prone bodies on the floor and stood by the door. "Come on," he said, "let's go."

I looked at him, wondering. Had he heard it too? Had the .357 jammed? Then, without volition, a flash from behind my eyes, and I saw it—I saw what could have been: the back of Mary Ellen's head reduced to a pulp of matted hair, blood and opened skull. Flecks of gray matter would have splattered my clothes; meat and bone would have been everywhere. I stood up, my heart fluttering wildly.

"Five minutes," I repeated. "Five minutes is all we ask." Then I said, "Let's go."

I let out a long, ragged breath. My knees were shaking as I opened the door and slid in front. Bruno, in back, was pale, but I knew the look of those eyes: we had done it. Eddie, laughing, drove.

I opened the glove compartment and took out the pill bottle. Two, three, four. I swallowed them dry and looked out into the desert as we followed the wind away from the bright lights.

CHAPTER FIFTEEN

Captured

We must have knocked over eight or ten of those large discount department stores in the six months we stayed together as a gang. Bruno and I were recognized by the others as the de facto leaders, putting together the strategies, casing the prospective targets, finding out when payrolls were delivered, and keeping the various tensions and rivalries that invariably spring up in such a partnership from interfering with our money - making ventures.

And money-making they were. Armed with an arsenal of weapons provided to us by dealers that Joey had put us in touch with, we established in that time a mini-reign of terror around the Southwestern region. Fifteen to twenty thousand dollars was not a bad take for five minutes work, split six ways. (Chest had brought in one of his friends early on to help cover the cash registers more effectively.) We were all making out very well.

Of course, for me, money meant just one thing—increased access to the drugs and booze that

had become my sole reason for existence. I guess
for awhile I was as anxious as any of my companions to live the high life—wining, dining, and
toting a huge wad of bills. But it soon became
apparent to me that there was really no one left to
impress. All the beautiful, willing women in the
world and all the fawning headwaiters and lavish
cars didn't add up to much when you couldn't pull
yourself together enough to take advantage of
them. I had even less reason to stay sober than in
Las Vegas; we would work no more than a few
minutes every other week, and the rest of the time
I was left to my own devices—deadly, poisonous
devices.

Gradually, with each successful robbery, the
security grid in the area became tighter. Stores
began hiring guards, credit offices were wired with
alarms, and money was moved out much more
quickly and under heavy surveillance. We were
going through our takes faster than we could pull
the jobs, and finding new ones was beginning to be
a problem. To meet the need we began robbing
smaller places (just for kicks more than anything
else), but splitting a few hundred dollars seven
ways hardly seemed worth the thrill. It was a
dangerous situation—seven desperate thieves with
no one to rob. The chances we took for the big
hauls became greater and greater.

Looking back to that time, it's amazing to me
that we didn't all get blown away in the act, or
worse, kill someone from sheer boredom. There
was a sense of cockiness in our outfit that breeds a
lethal carelessness. It was all too easy; everything
ran like clockwork, and the pulse-pounding thrill
of bucking the odds and hitting the big money was
beginning to pale. Petty quarrels started flaring up,

and Bruno, trying his best to hold things together, saw that it was time to move on.

I had been holed up in a cheap hotel room in downtown Phoenix for two or three weeks (the money from our last job was running low), waiting for word about the next heist. I had given up my role as planner and organizer with Bruno some time earlier. I simply couldn't be depended on to make meetings, think clearly, and come up with decent ideas. The night Bruno knocked on my door I was in the middle of a weeklong pill-and-bottle binge, and the time it took me to get up off the bed and answer the door must have helped him make up his mind.

"Gary, old buddy, you look like hell," he said, standing in the dim hallway light, smiling faintly. I'm not even sure I recognized him right away. I stood leaning against the doorjamb, trying to put his face in focus, wishing the flashing neon sign outside my window would stop casting its shadows on the wall. "I've got your cut," he said, reaching for his billfold.

Had an entire job passed me by? I was down to my last 20 bucks from a liquor store we'd hit a couple of weeks before, but for the life of me I couldn't remember past that.

"Cut," I mumbled. "Cut . . ."

"Gary, I want you to take this bread." He handed me a small stack of bills, but my fumbling fingers couldn't close on them. I watched them flutter to the floor like butterflies.

"I'll get it . . . ." I said, my words slurring and colliding with each other; "no problem . . . ." I tried to kneel, but the distance between my knees and the floor was too far. My legs folded under me, and as I went down I cracked my head on the doorjamb. All I heard was the noise; I couldn't feel a thing.

"You okay, Gary?" asked Bruno, kneeling down to help me off the floor, where I was crouching on all fours, my head lolling between my shoulders. I could smell his after-shave lotion and the crisp scent of his leather overcoat. Bruno always kept himself nice. Pushing him off with one hand, I mumbled something incoherent even to myself. I was okay—I just needed a minute down here where it was safe.

Then, without warning or volition, I vomited, bringing up volumes of clear liquid and small flecks of red matter. The money swam in the stinking pool. Bruno jumped back to avoid being splattered by a second onrush of sickness, and for a moment I found myself staring at his polished brogans.

From somewhere high above, he lit a cigarette. The smell of the vomit had cleared my head for the moment, and I realized for the first time since he arrived what was happening. I tried to get to my feet, but it was no good. I was just too weak.

"Don't bother," said Bruno, not unkindly. "Listen, Gary, the boys and I pulled a little job last night. Nothing spectacular, but I wanted you to get your share before . . ." his words trailed off. I think, on looking back, that he was genuinely sorry about what he had to do, despite the fact that I was groveling around at his feet, trying to keep my face out of my own sickness.

"Hold . . . on, just a minute, Bruno . . . ." I gasped, but it was obvious I wasn't getting to my feet any time soon.

"No, please, Gary, you'll be all right," he answered, and I felt his hand on my arm, pulling me up and guiding me back to the bed. Laying me gently down, Bruno went to the sink in the corner of the room and wet his handkerchief, dropping it gently across my forehead. It felt heavy and cold, but I was too weak to remove it.

A long silence ensued while Bruno gingerly fished the money out of the mess by the doorway and laid out the bills, one next to the other, on the nightstand to dry. My eyes were closed, but the sounds he was making went off like firecrackers in my head.

At last he was finished, and after washing his hands and drying them on the bedsheet, he leaned over me. I knew it without opening my eyes; I could feel him close to me.

"I tried to call you," he said softly, as if aware that every sound was a sharp agony; "but no one answered the phone." It was then that I half-remembered the tireless ring of the telephone next to my head, sometime, a long time ago. I had waited patiently for it to stop, and when it didn't I had finally curled a pillow over my head. When was it? It could have been yesterday or five years ago. I began testing myself—what was my name? How old was I? Where was I born? A sense of satisfaction grew as I recounted the facts to myself; I wasn't in such bad shape after all.

Bruno, meanwhile, was talking softly but urgently. "—did everything I could," he was saying when I finally tuned him back in. "But the boys insisted. You've gotta know that things are getting hot around here . . . Gary; Gary . . . are you listening?" I grunted. "Yeah, so we gotta move on. This nickel-and-dime routine is getting us nowhere."

"Just . . . gimme a minute," I said, sounding to myself as if I were in a vast, echoing tunnel. "I'll be with you in a minute . . ."

"No, Gary," Bruno replied, and his voice retreated as he got off the bed. I opened my eyes, squinting against the relentless neon light blinking on and off I made out his figure standing next to the bed. He was buttoning his overcoat. "I tried, but it's no good. The boys aren't having any of it. Chester's brother came down from Grand Rapids. We're moving out tonight."

"Moving out . . . tonight," I repeated dumbly. "I'll pack . . ."

"Gary, you got nothin' to pack," Bruno observed. "We're leaving you here. It's too big a risk, buddy. I'm sorry, but that's the way it goes. Chester's brother, he's good, he's got experience. We're moving' up north. San Francisco, maybe, or Seattle."

"San Francisco . . . pretty town," I muttered. My brain refused to function. I was feeling sick again.

"Yeah, it's beautiful. Take care of yourself, Gary." Bruno was standing by the door. "Adios."

"Gimme five minutes . . ." I said before dry heaving overwhelmed me. A long moment passed while I choked and gagged on the sweat-soaked bed. "Gimme five . . . ." But there was no one left to wait for me.

Sick, penniless, and completely alone, I found myself, a month later, with only one friend: the .357 magnum I had used during my crime spree. I had long since been tossed out of the hotel, and on that blistering hot August night I spent the last of the 400 dollars that Bruno had left me. I cursed him for being such a cheapskate, my violent swearing bouncing off the dirty brick walls of the narrow alley where I nursed the last of a bottle of cheap port wine. My half-articulated shouts woke others, who swore back at me in Spanish or talked to themselves until oblivion once again drowned their voices. A cat moved across my field of vision, sniffing at garbage cans. It was skinny and its fur was matted and stiff. Pulling the gun from the pocket of my filthy suit (the only thing left to me from my former high-rolling days), I took careful aim and pulled the trigger. A blinding flash of light and a deafening roar slammed against me, pushing me into a cardboard box full of bottles and tin cans, which cascaded down, rattling and shattering over me.

My companions in the alley staggered to their feet in bewilderment and confusion. those who in the half-light could see the gun in my hand made themselves quickly scarce or hid, whispering Hail Mary's. The cat, I noticed with satisfaction, was a mangled lump of fur and bone at the far end of the alley. I still had it, I told myself; there was nothing wrong with me.

Except the lack of a bottle. I needed something to drink, could feel the need creeping up my throat, constricting my breathing, stuffing my mouth with cotton. Getting to my feet, I tucked the pistol in my belt and staggered out onto the street, still bustling with activity—pool halls, prostitutes, all-night diners, and drunks.

I hated it all. If I had enough bullets, I thought to myself, I would put them all out of their misery. They didn't deserve to live. How could they stand to look at themselves and each other? This was hell, if ever there was such a place, and I needed a belt to make it go away.

It was then that I saw the hamburger stand, a miserable-looking joint on the corner, blazing with harsh white light, but empty. No wonder, I thought to myself—look at it. Greasy and filthy, it made me sick to think of eating there, that other people ate there, paid money to gobble down burgers and stare at the flyspecked wallpaper. As I came closer I saw the woman behind the counter, and my hate and loathing found its target.

Inside, the ugly old cow took my order. I despised her as she moved off on her tree-trunk legs, taking her own sweet time. Burger, fries, and a Coke. What was so hard about that? But she had made me repeat it twice. That was something she would pay for.

Did she have any idea who she was talking to? No, of course not; if she did, she would be slobbering in fear, her fat face coming apart in animal terror, knowing that any second, like lightning, with a simple twitch of my finger, I could dispatch her to the fate she deserved. Instead, she just turned around, her thin, gray hair falling in wisps around her pocked face, the sleeveless print dress stained with grease and sweat. She wiped the sweat with a rag next to the grill and watched absently as the patty sizzled away. It was more, in that jangled, overheated moment, than I could bear.

I pulled the gun from my belt and told her to turn around, smiling that look of dumb resignation turned pale and quaking in the space of a moment. I waved the barrel at the cash register. Opening it, she pulled out a pitiful handful of bills—it couldn't have been more than 30 bucks. I considered wasting her then and there, but a better idea came to me—a little joke, something to remember me by.

I told her to finish the order, and laughed as her trembling hands fought to put the patty on the bun and spread the mustard and catsup. She spilled the Coke and burned herself as she scooped the fries.

The paper bag was already stained with grease spots as I turned to leave, the bills stuffed in my jacket pocket. As I swung around, the first thing I saw were their service revolvers leveled at me. The next thing that caught my eye were their badges. "I used to have one just like them" was the thought that went through my skull. The cops had to pry my hands off the bag full of food as they slapped the cuffs on my wrists and hustled me into the back of the squad car.

CHAPTER SIXTEEN

The State Pen

I wanted to get caught; I *had* to get caught. There was no choice; it was a simple matter of survival. There comes a point in the life of an alcoholic, or a drug addict, or a person who in any way has completely lost control, when self-will fails and the instinct for self-preservation takes control. It may seem odd that my will to live chose arrest and incarceration as a way to assert itself. To me it points up the simple fact that our subsconscious, untapped mental processes are often much more sophisticated than we give them credit for.

I spent six months in the Maricopa County Jail awaiting trial—six months of resting, eating right, drying out, and slowly returning to a state of health I hadn't known in years. I gained weight, the awful gauntness of my face receded, and in its place came a man I barely recognized in the mirror every morning. I don't remember doing a lot of thinking in that time; I had no remorse or guilt, no questions about my future, no resolve to do better. I was in a holding pattern, a kind of dreamlike state, letting nature do her healing work.

The county jail itself was a decent enough place compared to where I'd been, and certainly to where I was going. It was clean, the food was half-decent, and my "roommates" were of a transient nature, usually just stopping over on their way to somewhere, and not ready to make trouble for me. There were drunks, petty thieves, pimps, and even an occasional rapist and murderer, but I never really had to deal with them; I wasn't obligated to form friendships, chew the fat, and establish my territory. I was just there—another guy down on his luck, whose face reflected nothing more than a mild curiosity as to where his next cigarette was coming from.

My drug and liquor demons were also quiescent during this half-year healing period. I knew I wasn't going to be getting high; the county jail, unlike other similar institutions, didn't allow for the usual fraternization between guards and inmates, a fraternization that results in contraband for sale or trade. It was strictly business, and somehow the destructive habits of a lifetime were temporarily put on hold. It was the closest to being a vegetable that I can imagine, adjusting my inner clock to the routine: lights on, lights off, three meals, exercise. I could have continued like that for years and never even noticed the passage of time.

But of course time did pass, and with it the arrival of my day in court. By the time I stood before the judge, I looked better than I had at any time since my days as a police officer. My face was scrubbed and I stood clean-shaven in a fresh pair of prison overalls. Along with my refurbished appearance, something of my old charm had returned. I was polite to the court, eloquent in my repentance, fervent in my promise to reform, and anguished over the error of my ways. I looked and sounded, to all the world, like a man who had come to this senses after a long and debilitating illness.

Whether it was my well-acted show before His Honor, or my past as a policeman, or my heretofore-spotless record, or my Masonic membership (the judge himself was a Freemason of some standing), or a combination of them all, I'll never know. Whatever it was, I got off light: three years of probation, with some very specific conditions. There was to be no association with my old cronies, no drinking or drugs, and gainful employment at the first available opportunity. With every well-turned phrase and contrite expression I could muster, I promised to be a good boy. They cut me loose.

Three days later I woke up in a vacant lot at the far end of town, drenched in my own urine and clutching a bottle of port in my hand. I had no job and no money, and if I could have found Bruno I would have been glad to hit a liquor store to get enough for a handful of pills. So much for six months of solemn sobriety. But this time that same dogged instinct for suvival wouldn't allow me to sink back into the morass I had so recently emerged from. Climbing to my feet, I made my way downtown to the office of my probation officer. He rearrested me on the spot, and a sentence of three to five years for grand larceny (knocked down in court from armed robbery) was imposed. I would serve my time in the Arizona State Penitentary.

Alcatraz Island, in the middle of a freezing expanse of water, forlorn and forbidding, has nothing on the Arizona State Pen. For every mile of water that separates a con from freedom at the Rock, there are ten miles of God-forsaken, lethal desert wasteland between the Alcatraz of the Desert and civilization. The view from the wall at the Arizona State Penitentary is no view at all; it is flat in every direction; scrub brush and barrel cactus keep a silent guard over the bitter emptiness; desolation is the constant companion to loneliness. Coyotes, horned toads, and Gila monsters are the citizens of the expanse.

And there, in the exact center of this awesome and hellish wasteland, are the looming adobe walls of the Joint. Its building and recreation yard are the same drab color as the desert rock; the prison must have been old and crumbling the day it was finished. The settlement of trustee huts huddle like slumbering quail beneath the shadow of the big house. It is the kind of place to which a man comes to die, and it was death or the fear of it that was in my mind that simmering morning I passed through the towering main gates of the place to begin my term as a number, in a row, on a block, doing hard time.

I had had a few weeks back in the county jail to dry out from my last binge—the one that brought me out of the frying pan and into this very real fire—and I was thinking clearly as they unloaded us from the wagon and into a holding tank, waiting for processing. I was thinking too clearly for my own taste; I could have used a stiff belt to blur the edges of this harsh reality a little, a couple of pills or a snort of powder to lift the oppressive atmosphere that lingered over the place.

As they stripped and searched us one by one, I noted every small detail of the place, and each

detail increased the fear that had settled on me
from the moment I laid eyes on the place. Things
could happen to you here, things that no one likes
to talk about, things that you may not live to tell
about. Sure, my urge to survive had forced me off
the streets, but what it had driven me to was a far
more insidious existence. Around every corner,
behind every face, at any given moment of any
given day lurked a potential for drawing your last
breath of life.

Seeing the casual sadism on the faces of the
guards, brutalized and hardened by a miserable job
with lousy pay and absolutely no future, noticing
the way the older cons checked each of us out as we
passed naked down a line toward a perfunctory
medical exam and the issuance of our gray prison
uniforms, sensing the tension, the undercurrent of
violence and cruelty that clotted the already
heatladen air, I knew I had come to a point in my
checkered career when all the odds were against
me. The desire to do myself in had for once been
taken out of my hands. Any one of the prisoners in
this monument to despair (there was little difference between inmates and guards in this
place—all were victims of a system that destroyed
people wholesale) would as soon kill me as look at
me. These were men who had nothing to lose; the
lifers, the three-time losers, the psychos, the career
guards, the trustees, the officials all the way up to
the warden. Everyone had succumbed to the dehumanization that was symbolized by this towering
edifice in the midst of a blighted landscape.

It was hot, miserably hot, and the smell of
cramped humanity stung our nostrils and made it
impossible to take a deep breath. After we were
processed and dressed, the horror of the place grew

as we were led down an endless corridor toward the "fish tank"—that block of cells reserved for the new inmates. As we made our way under the bored gaze of rifle-toting guards further and further into the bowels of that place, the thought of existing in such a world seemed hopeless. The air grew ever more stale—the smells, excrement, sweat, and cigarette smoke brought a sudden rush of nausea. Light yielded to dimness as the corridor's feeble electric bulbs grew farther and farther apart. We passed a myriad of cellblocks branching off this main corridor like cancerous growths. Glimpses of men on the cellblock floor, playing cards, reading, staring out at us or into the gray distance, flitted by at regular intervals. There was no doubt about it—I had arrived in hell for the punishment I deserved.

That night I lay in my bunk, listening to the sounds coming from the tier of cells above us. This area was reserved for the prison's more blatant homosexuals, those repeated sexual offenders who had to be isolated from the main area because of their insatiable sexual appetites. Hooting and jeering, they shouted down to us what we might expect from them once they got hold of us. It was horrifying, a depiction of perversity in detail graphic enough to put a cold sweat on my skin despite the stifling heat. They spurred each other on to more and more elaborate descriptions of what we could look forward to, while below I heard the lazy laughter of guards.

It seemed to go on forever. As soon as one would run out of steam, another would pick up the flood of invectives and filth; it was like drowning in a human sewer. Every evil urge to which the flesh is prone, every variety of sexual disorder, everything one man could conceive of to do to another, was given voice in that thick darkness.

I haven't read much of what they call the classics; I'm not too familiar with how great poets and writers of the past have described hell and the torments of sinners. But after that night, I don't need to. Dante's *Inferno* could only be a pale echo of the "fishtank" on a July night. It was then that the realization of just how far I had sunk came over me. I began sobbing, my body shaking and trembling like a leaf, tears mixing with sweat to soak my face and the stale mattress I was lying on. I was looking for a word, a name, something to call out for, to hold onto. I felt then that death would be preferable to what had become of me. As the leering dialogue went on above me, I fell asleep and dreamed of home, somewhere far off and long ago.

CHAPTER SEVENTEEN

The "Fish"

Duties for the "fish" were designed to stamp out whatever spark of rebellion was left in the newcomers, whether it was against the authority with uniforms and guns or the authorities living next to them in the tiny, airless cells. Anyone who has been in prison for a stretch can testify to the fact that more often than not it's the inmates, those with power and pull, who actually run the place. At Arizona State it was an extreme case. We were all in it together, guards and cons, hundreds of miles from anything. But at least the inmates—most of them, anyway—had release dates to look forward to.

For the guards, it was low pay, long hours, and a life sentence, or retirement, whichever came first. It was no wonder they were so easy to bribe for all sorts of special treatment and favors. They were anxious, really, demanding their due from newcomers, exchanging money sent from the outside for drugs, liquor, and special privileges that included everything from letting homosexual lovers visit each other's cells at night to ignoring a gang rape in the shower.

There was, of course, no money in prison. What money you had was sent to you from relatives and friends—my dad, in my case—and put on account at the prison store. The medium of exchange inside was cigarettes; you could get just about anything in the yard or on the block for a pack of cigarettes, and nearly all the funds I received from outside eventually went toward carton upon carton of smokes.

But the savvy required to work the system to my advantage was a long time in coming. It's appropriate, I think, that new inmates were called "fish" by guards and cons alike. It was most definitely survival of the fittest behind those walls, and the big fish ate the little ones without a second thought.

My first job, along with those who had come in with me, was picking cotton in the fields behind the trustee settlement. It was blistering, miserable stoop labor, hunched over all day beneath an absolutely merciless sun and watched over by guards on horses. The backbreaking, humiliating labor was intended to drain a man of his last ounce of energy and self-respect. I hated it from the moment I was handed the long, narrow bag that dragged behind me on the ground and that never seemed to fill up, matter how many bolls I yanked off their stems.

It was in the fields, on my very first day out, sweating and aching, that I ran across Buddy. Buddy had been with me in the Maricopa County Jail, sent up for auto theft, and was facing the same three-to-five-years sentence I was. But Buddy had made a terrible mistake shortly after he had arrived, some three weeks before I did.

He was a young man, tall and slender, and I recognized him immediately even though his face was turned down and the shadow of his straw hat obscured his features. He was working the row next to me, silently and intently, picking, it seemed to me, as if his life depended on it.

"Buddy!" I said, genuinely glad to see a familiar face. "Man, you're a sight for sore eyes!" The fact was, I hadn't spoken three words to him the whole time we were together in county jail, but out there in that cotton field he could have been my dear departed mother.

It was when he looked up, straight into my face, that my expression melted into one of shock and horror. His young features, finely chiseled and expressive, had now become the focus for a horrible deformity: his left eye was nothing but a gaping socket, dark and shriveled. The fiery light in his remaining good eye served only to bring the empty hole into sharper relief.

I must have said something like "My God!" or "What happened?" I don't really remember. More likely, I just stood there in utter disbelief, staring at his young face, forever marred.

"Kelly," was all he said to me before turning furiously back to his work, and he spat the name like it was poisonous fire in his mouth. Kelly. I found out later what had happened. Buddy, after a few days out of the fish tank, had witnessed a rape in the showers one morning. It was his misfortune to have been there at all, but he compounded his mistake by reporting the incident to a guard. Later that day, in the yard, a beefy lifer known as Henry had walked up to him, dug this thumb into Buddy's socket, and plucked the eye out onto the dusty concrete. "That's what happens," he whispered as Buddy clutched his face in agony, blood pouring down his arm, "to squealers."

This hideous object lesson had been at the direct orders of Kelly, a three-time loser, serving a life sentence for kidnapping and murder. Kelly was one of the big fish, maybe the biggest in the joint at the time. He had a squad of lieutenants who enforced his reign by maiming, threatening, and strong-arming the population into submission. Kelly was the kind of man who, through ruthlessness and cruelty, established complete dominance in whatever environment he found himself. It would have been the same on the streets; he was a cutthroat kingpin with an army of goons, for whom places like Arizona State Pen had been built in the first place. He was busy teaching everyone the bottom line: submit or suffer the consequences. There wasn't a guard in the place who didn't owe Kelly something—money, favors, some outside connection—that made their life a little easier. He was the undisputed master of the joint, a king rat of an infested mountain with a scepter of terror and fear.

He was also a rabid homosexual and had been so for as long as anyone could remember. That, of course, wasn't unusual for someone who had spent as much of his life behind bars as Kelly; what was unusual was the way in which he enforced his wishes and desires. His was an indisputable law, as I was to discover soon enough.

That evening, when the sun, by some blessed act of mercy, finally dipped below the horizon, we were marched to a weighing station off to the side of the field. One by one we hauled our long bags, hanging from our shoulders like some burden of guilt, up to the scales. There, a guard lazily checked the weight of our day's labor, and if it met the minimum requirement, we next pulled it to a large wire bin where we painstakingly emptied the cotton fluffs. It was incredible to me that something as light and insubstantial as a boll of cotton could, when multiplied thousands of times, become as heavy as a weight of pig iron.

Mine was heavy, but not heavy enough. As I pulled my bag onto the rusty scale, the guard suddenly perked up. Looking at me, he made a note of my number on a clipboard and asked me my name.

"Been sleeping out there, Bell?" he sneered. I kept silent, biting my tongue. I felt like putting *him* to sleep at the bottom of my bag, suffocating him in a swarm of cotton, but I stood there instead, looking at my feet, for all the world like a slave before his master. "Move on, Bell," he said, but I knew this wasn't the end of the incident. I hadn't picked enough cotton and could only speculate at what the prescribed discipline was for such an offense.

I found out soon enough. On returning to the cellblock, as tired as I could ever remember being in my life, I was called out of the line by the bull in charge. He ordered me to strip down, and from behind his desk he pulled a wooden crate, the kind used to pack soft drinks. Gesturing for me to follow him, he took the crate and set it, on edge, in the middle of the block.

"Get up," he said. I looked at him without comprehension. "Climb up, stupid," he shouted, pointing at the box. "Maybe after a night on that you'll pick a little faster."

I climbed on the box, struggling for a moment to maintain my balance, and then stood stark naked while around me the gossip, card games, and normal prison routine continued. The dinner bell rang and, single file, the cons marched off to the mess hall, leaving me alone on a box whose dimensions seemed to be shrinking by the moment. I was already exhausted from my day in the field, filled quotient or not, and the effort of staying perched on the side of that wooden crate very shortly caused my body to shriek for relief. But I knew better; I kept thinking of Buddy, his hollow socket staring me down. If it could happen to him, who knows what might happen to me if I didn't remain here like some obscene statue in a park? I didn't dare find out.

It was just about lock-in time, that point in the prison routine when the inmates are locked in their cells for the night, when a balding, obese man came up to me where I stood, trembling and sweating. He spent a long moment in front of me, casting an admiring glance over my body, winking lewdly when my eyes caught his.

"I like you," he said. "What's your name, boy?" I knew then without anyone telling me—this was Kelly. It was a matter of his presence, a feel about the man that reflected his own sense of power and control. He was sizing me up like a side of beef. Swallowing against the lump in my throat, I kept silent.

Our exchange hadn't gone unnoticed on the cellblock floor. Conversation gradually fell silent, eyes turned to where I stood, and anxious whispers could be heard.

"I asked you your name, boy," Kelly repeated, still smiling. My defiance was nothing more than amusing to him. A small, ratty-looking con with a broken nose came up behind him.

"You want I should make him show some respect, boss?" he asked in a nasal voice. Kelly seemed to consider the offer while I tried to keep my knees from shaking.

"No," he said finally, "I don't think so. This guy thinks he's tough. That's good. I tell you what, tough guy, I'm makin' an appointment with you. Tomorrow, the showers, let's say 7:00. That'll give you some time to think about what happens to guys who don't keep their appointments." He reached out, taking hold of a pinch of flesh on my thigh, nodding approvingly, as if I had passed some test for firmness and tenderness.

I had to decide right then and there. I knew that if I didn't at least try to assert myself right away, the problem would never go away. I wasn't going to let this guy use me, no matter what. The question was, would I spend my time trying to avoid the inevitable, or face it down now? Thinking of Buddy and the kind of law Kelly laid down, I made up my mind. It was no good any other way. I had to stand up to him, regardless of the cost.

In a single movement I leaped off the crate, and as it clattered behind me I pushed my fist into Kelly's face, knocking him down and sending me sprawling on top of him. I didn't waste a moment, but kept pummeling away at his head and neck, shouting and swearing, clawing at his flesh, drawing blood and shrieks of pain.

It took two guards to drag me off him, and one more to haul me down to the basement and to the six-by-eight nightmare called solitary.

CHAPTER EIGHTEEN

Solitary Confinement

I spent ten days that first time in solitary confinement—ten days in a room so black I couldn't see my hand in front of my face, ten days in nothing but my underwear and a skimpy cotton blanket, ten days trying to force down food so vile my stomach simply couldn't accept it despite my growing hunger. There was nothing in that stifling closet but a roll of toilet paper and a hole in the corner—no mattress, no chair, no company except the roaches crawling over my body when I'd awake from long, dreamless sleep.

Time moved slowly or not at all; there was nothing to gauge the passage of days—no lengthening shadows, no moon or stars or change in the weather, no small talk, no occupying habits, no consuming details to mark one moment from the next. It was just me, alone with myself, and after a few days I made the worst company imaginable. That first time in the airless closet, clogged with the smell of my own vomit, it wasn't the loneliness or the sensory deprivation or the timelessness that got to me the most; it was the boredom.

After my term in the hole I was released into the general prison population and began serving my time in earnest. I was shortly transferred out of the fish tank, off the cotton-picking detail, and into the prison hospital, as a ward nurse, administering medicine, cleaning bedpans, and changing sheets. I must say, I wasn't much surprised, after a few months, to see a familiar face turn up. Bruno had taken a fall—armed robbery. It seemed that having him there was the completion of a long cycle—the high life of Vegas, our desperado days together in Phoenix, and now this. What else could have happened? It had a strange and final logic to it, a kind of poetic justice that I acknowledged without really understanding why. I accepted this as the inevitable result of the life we had led, like some mathematical equation that, when all the factors are added together, can equal only one possible sum. For us, the sum was this citadel in the desert.

Of course I was happy to have a friend among so many hostile and potentially dangerous strangers, particularly since Bruno had a talent that made him well-valued in the prison population, and by securing a job as his assistant I fell under the protective wing of that skill. The Doctor's surgical abilities were worth their weight in gold, or at least cigarettes. Bruno could sew up knife wounds, remove cysts, and perform circumcisions with a professional's ease, and he was well-paid for his services. It was a largesse he shared with me, his old partner in crime, and for the time I assisted him I was as comfortable and safe as anyone could be in such a place.

That favored position didn't last for long, thanks to my old urge for getting high. When the prison pharmacist was taken sick, I was assigned temporary duty dispensing drugs—the equivalent of letting a kid loose in a well-stocked candy store. For every two pills I gave out I set aside three for myself, not caring particularly what they were, just knowing that together and in combination I could get temporarily out of my mind.

Arizona State was no exception to just about any other prison in the country as far as availability of drugs and alcohol was concerned. Cigarettes could get you a snort of heroin, a bottle of Scotch, marijuana, speed, downers—whatever the market could bear. I wasn't rich enough to maintain my old habits (no one in the joint was), but I was able to satisfy an occasional whim now and then if only to relieve the tedium. It's remarkable to me, looking back, how my addictions, constrained by circumstances, suited themselves to availability. Without the means to drink constantly, my alcoholism went into a dormant stage—not disappearing, but simply hibernating.

Take my stint as the prison druggist. Before I landed the job, I would trade the occasional pack of smokes for a pill or two, just for something to do. I knew I could never get enough to sataisfy my real appetite for the stuff, so I was content with what I could get, when I could get it. But as soon as I had access to significant amounts in the pharmacy, the hoary old beast raised its ugly head again and I became a bona fide drug freak.

It couldn't and didn't last. They knew what I was up to, if not from the missing inventory, then certainly from my saucer eyes and the smile plastered on my face. I was pulled from the hospital in short order and sent down to work in the clothing factory, where uniforms were manufactured from the cotton we picked. I had, as usual, blown a good thing.

Working the looms and sewing machines of the factory was about a half-step up from the field-hand work I had begun my term with. It was hot, noisy, and dangerous work. It was dangerous because it was not as heavily supervised as other shops, and thus it was a much more likely place to get stabbed, raped, or beaten up for some infraction, real or imagined. The sprawling factory took up an entire floor, with machines rattling and churning incessantly, providing plenty of nooks and crannies as well a substantial cover of noise under which all sorts of nasty deeds could be committed.

I had no idea what my standing was with Kelly and his hierarchy, and while I suspected I wouldn't be the brunt of his sexual advances anymore, I couldn't be sure that I wasn't the target of some kind of terminal vengeance at the hands of one of his underlings. I had been relatively safe from such threats while working in the hospital; no one wanted to get on Bruno's bad side for fear that they might one day require his specialized services, and the working environment was a lot smaller and better supervised. In the clothing shop anything could happen and, more often than not, did. The kind of paranoia I had every right to experience didn't help the time fly by. I was always looking over my shoulder, at the hands of other cons—expecting to see the dull glint of a homemade knife—or into shadows and corners, half-expecting figures to leap out at me with murder in their eyes. Murder, when it finally came, appeared from an unexpected direction, setting off a chain of events that nearly killed me in the process.

I was rounding the six-month mark of my sentence; translated into prison time, this meant that nearly a third of my stint was up. I had been sentenced to three to five years, which in legal parlance meant the low figure, providing I kept my nose clean and didn't make things difficult for the powers that be. If I worked while serving my term (there wasn't any choice in that—if you were an inmate you had to work), one day was counted as two; in other words, I was actually serving half my sentence—18 months. Life in the joint had taken on a predictable if unpleasant routine. There is perhaps nothing more demeaning than working, and working hard, for nothing. The only thing that's worse is working for 35-cents-a-day wage we were "paid" in prison. Hauling heavy bolts of cloth, running a seam down a pair of pant legs all day long—this kind of work was dehumanizing enough. The added insult of slaving literally for pennies made it almost unendurable. Of course, unendurable is just a word; what else was there to do but endure, count the days, and try to subdue the hatred that boiled up in your gut from time to time?

I was toting a cart full of bolts of the blue denim that would be turned into work uniforms. As I pushed the load down the long central passageway between the pounding machines of the shop, my progress was slowed by two cons walking with a deliberate pace, side by side, towards the guard station in the center of the floor. The station was a glassed-in cubicle holding a couple of chairs and a table where the day's figures were added by a pair of guards. Both guards, a lieutenant and his captain, were inside, smoking cigarettes and playing cards. As the two cons approached the station, the phone rang soundlessly against the roar of the shop. The captain answered, exchanged a word with the lieutenant, and walked out the door and down the aisle on some errand at the other end of the floor. The two in front of me stopped and watched. There was something strange in their actions, and I observed closely as one of them summoned the remaining guard with a shout and a gesture. I recognized the two then; they both worked for Kelly, and were both homosexual lovers who had been separated by a cell tier when their behavior became too blatant.

In the few seconds it took the lieutenant to make his way down the aisle (the captain, meanwhile, was conferring with a con near one of the looms), I knew something was about to happen; it was a feeling like static electricity in the air. The dull roar of the machines seemed miles away and the scene before my eyes took on the dimensions of a ritual drama being played out in minute and horrific detail. If I could have I would have turned away, looked in the other direction; I would have been infinitely better off for it, but it was no use. I was hypnotized by what was going to happen. Like a spectator at some gruesome blood sport, the scent of the impending kill kept me spellbound. I watched while in seeming slow motion the con nearest the young, baby-faced lieutenant drew a short, homemade blade from the waistband of his pants. With a single, fluid thrust, the shiv entered the belly of the guard, and with a vicious movement to the right the con pulled the sharpened edge, drawing a long, clean line across his abdomen.

For a breathless moment nothing happened. Then, with dizzying speed, chaotic action crowded in on me. The pounding of the machines all around returned, and in the blink of an eye the two murderous cons had vanished into thin air. I watched as blood gushed from the gaping wound in the guard's stomach and he crumpled soundlessly to the floor. There I stood, my hands still on the cart, stiff and motionless, unable to credit what my eyes had just witnessed. I had come close to killing people in my career—maiming and crippling were certainly within the realm of my experience—but this was the first time I had seen a human life dispatched so swiftly and ruthlessly. The knowledge that in the space of a single breath a living being had been snuffed out was, more than anything else, amazing to me. I remember distinctly thinking how fragile and vulnerable men were. If that was all it took . . . just will, motivated by hate. It was as if the con had destroyed his enemy with a glance of an eye—it was that quick, that casual, that irrevocable.

I looked up finally from the figure leaking life over the filthy floor. The first thing I saw was the captain rushing up to me as I stood alone next to the body, his face reflecting a furious question.

"Who did it, Bell?" he asked, kneeling over the body and holding the useless, limp wrist of the dead man. I looked at him, my lips pursed, hardly daring to breathe.

He swore, "Who did this, Bell?" I shook my head and shrugged. The blood was beginning to form a pool at my feet. I took a step backward as the captain rose. "I'm going to ask you one more time, Bell. Who did this?" The machinery roared relentlessly on.

I knew better. The code of honor, if that's what you want to call it, of prison life forbade the telling of such an awful secret. No matter what was in store for me, I couldn't name the names he wanted to hear. If I did, the code would be breached and my life would have been worth less than the dead body that lay at my feet. Maybe I thought I was actually being noble; that was one way of coping with the awful fear that gripped me as I looked into the captain's eyes. Maybe I thought I was upholding the unwritten law of the con, a law that seals the lips not for the sake of friendship or loyalty but from fear. It was the old, tired game of survival. I didn't know what was going to happen to me at the hands of the enraged guard, coldly determined to avenge the death of his lieutenant, but I did know what would happen to me at the hands of those who had done this monstrous deed. The unknown chance was by far the preferable option. I shook my head again and stood silent as he summoned help to take me downstairs.

It was 28 days this time, 28 days in total, consuming darkness. If ten days of deprivation had taxed my abilities to keep the goal of survival in sight, then that interminable purgatory I suffered took me past all thought of myself and all ability to reason, plan or hope. As bad as the food was—a foul slop they pushed under the door once a day—I would gladly have eaten it, if only I remembered how. If there was something in my past or future to keep my mind alert and functioning, I gladly would have focused on it. There was nothing. If there was some burning emotion to fan the flames of hate or vengeance, I surely would have allowed it to gain full control. Everything flickered and was extinguished like a candle in an airless jar. I was no longer human, no longer even really alive. My body continued to function—I drew breath, my heart beat, my eyes blinked—but it was for no reason. Death was the same as life; darkness was the same as light; I was reduced to something between an animal and mute, inanimate object—a rock or a piece of wood.

To be sure, at first I tried everything to keep hold of my sanity. I played endless games with myself, trying to remember the street I had lived on as a child in Chicago, the address, how many houses on the block, and the name of each family. I would trace my steps to school and spend hours trying to recall the names of all my schoolmates—where they sat in the classroom and the color of their hair. I would recount all the characters of my favorite childhood radio program, hear their voices vividly in my mind, remember specific episodes, even strain to recount the dialogue. I followed by rote each stage of my miserable life, lingering over every small detail—not for remonstrance or remorse, but simply to hold onto the simple fact that I *was* somebody. I had a name, a face, a history.

Gradually, however, it began to slip away. At first I found myself sleeping for longer and longer periods of time, waking up exhausted and disoriented, only to fall into deeper and deeper slumber for longer periods of time. This was followed by intermittent periods of delirium, episodes where I wouldn't be in the stinking hole at all, but in a field of clover, in my mother's arms, or sitting in a cool bar on a balmy night sipping double Scotch. When I'd come out of these fragmentary escapes, I would fear for my sanity, trying desperately to evoke something solid, pinching myself, butting my head against a wall, pulling my hair, which, like my teeth, was beginning to loosen from lack of nutrition. Inevitably, however, I would slip back into sleep and wake not knowing who or where I was. It was a cycle that brought with it a blessed kind of unconsciousness, and soon I gave up trying to reassert reality; the dreams and fantasies were so much more pleasent, so much more soothing and comforting.

The last thing I remember experiencing in the darkness was a vivid dream of my dad and me walking the streets of our old neighborhood. He held my hand and I skipped along beside him, happy and secure. I was wearing knickers and he was telling me about the baseball game we were going to. It was the Cubs against the Dodgers. He, of course, was rooting for the home team, but had to admit that the boys from Brooklyn had some fine pitching. I wanted him to buy me some peanuts and a Cubs pennant. Laughing, he took me in his arms and there on the street hugged me tightly, kissed me on the forehead, and told me how very much he loved me.

When I regained consciousness I was out of the black hole, lying on an indescribably soft bed, the smell of clean sheets in my nostrils. Was I dreaming? Had I died? I had no way of knowing that they had at last come for me, taken me from the tormenting hell where I had been dying for a month, and brought me, delirious and weak from malnutrition, into the prison infirmary. All I knew was that I was out, that dead or alive I had passed the ultimate test of my stamina. Whatever happened now could never be as bad as the everlasting darkness through which I had just emerged.

The bed where I lay faced a window which looked out on the prison yard. It was late afternoon and the Southwestern sun shone over the adobe wall, through the window and onto my face. As I opened my eyelids, the full rays of the sun fell upon eyes, which had not seen light for 28 days. With a terrifying shriek of agony, a pain like molten metal on the tender optiac nerves sent me reeling into the profound night of total blindness, back to where I had been.

CHAPTER NINETEEN

Back to Life and Death

When I saw her stepping off the bus, her light summer dress blowing in the breeze, the small child in knee socks and shined shoes clinging to her hand, it was perhaps the happiest, most contented moment of my miserable life. The smile that dazzled me through the swirl of people in the station, the warmth of her hand in mine as we walked out into the street hailing a cab in the balmy Los Angeles afternoon—these are sensations that have never left me. There was no cause that day to fear, no reason to lie or scheme. I had found her again. Her calm, her strength flowed into me lifted me up, and gave me for the first time in as long as I could remember some hope for the future. It could be all right, things could still work out, if only she would stay with me.

There were no questions that had to be answered, no vows to be made or assurances sought. She loved me as I loved her. She had held onto something these long years and I realized then that I had too. Even when I could call no thought or emotion my own, somewhere, deeply buried but firmly anchored, I held out the hope, like a beacon against the raging night. What was shared knew no passage of time or trial. It was as if we had just met again, both still working in the bank, a fragile feeling between us nurtured as something unspoken grew.

What neither of us could say, we both knew—we were in love. The child of our shame had become the proof of our bond, and I had, after a lifetime of suffering, returned to claim what was mine: Dorothy, my future wife, and Janet, my daughter.

We spoke all through the night that first visit. She answered my phone call, a tentative and faltering contact, and she had come as if I summoned her directly. I knew as she stepped down from the bus and sought my eyes, drawn by some unfathomable magnetic power. that we were to be man and wife. It was a promise unspoken and understood.

We talked of the past without evasion, as if we were finally laying down some tremendous burden. She told me of her life with John, the sense of lack, an emptiness that grew as the years dragged on. She asked that I believe her when she told me of her certainty that we would someday be together as man and wife, and I did. She knew, she said, very little of me or what had happened in my life. All she could see as we sat in the small hours of the morning in my father's apartment, while in the next room Janet slept the deep sleep of childhood—all she could tell was that I was tired, that I needed rest and someplace to lay my head.

If I could have wept I would, but another urgency crowded out the tears—the need to confess everything to her. I confessed all that had happened, without exception, watching her face with the breathless anticipation that the next revelation might break the bond between us. Yet the work that love had started in us could only be revealed in completeness, and Dorothy was far too wise, far too certain to allow the sins of the past to destroy the blessings of the future.

I had, in time, recovered from my blindness in prison, and eventually was transferred to a clerking job outside the walls in the trustee settlement. It was there that I passed the remainder of my sentence. Each day marked meticulous progress toward my freedom, but as far as my appreciation of that freedom, once attained, I would have been better off serving a life sentence behind the dull bars. As it was, I merely traded, readily and without a second thought, one prison for another.

I was given parole and remanded to the custody of my father, living then in Los Angeles. I sought and was granted permission to make a one night stopover in Phoenix to visit Darlene and Jerri. A more sour and uncordial reception would be hard to imagine. As soon as I got off the bus I bought a fifth of vodka with some of the money I had so laboriously earned in near-slave-labor in prison. With half the bottle in my belly, I paid a visit to my former wife, now living in a small house at the edge of town. We all went out for a Mexican dinner, eaten hurriedly and in stony silence, and the goodbyes we exchanged when they dropped me off were sincere only because we all wanted them to be forever. I had made a stupid, if typical mistake in thinking that part of my past could be dusted off and set aright. Too much that was ugly and dangerous had passed between Darlene and me, it poisoned even the joy I felt at seeing my beloved Jerri again.

Seeing my father cheered me up considerably, although for him the omens were ominous. I turned up on his doorstep drunk, and within three days I had run through all my prison savings and a good chunk of money that he had lent me "until I got a job." I think by then we both saw the writing on the wall—there wasn't going to be a job, a new leaf, or a fresh start. Eighteen months in Arizona State had simply been an extended breathing spell for me. I was back to drinking with all the fervor that my renewed good health provided me.

There was, of course, little that my father could do. Blood is, after all, thicker than water. Could he throw me out again on my own, considering what had happened to me the last time? Could he let me take that awful plunge into degeneracy, crime, and horrendous self-abuse without at least trying to provide me with every chance? It was, of course, guilt that motivated him—the guilt that any parent feels when a child goes astray. Was it something in the way the child was raised, in the values he was taught? The answer, for me, was no. I brought on myself every last measure of pain and grief, but there are few enough certainties in this world, and the comfort that a parent might feel at the certainty of knowing that he is not ultimately responsible for his child is granted very rarely. My Dad suffered, and by his suffering he brought more on himself.

I, of course, was oblivious to all of this. I had, in fact, begun a cycle that was to last the better part of the next three years: unchecked binges, followed by complete loss of control, followed by a stint in a clinic, sanatorium, hospital, or mental ward; a drying-out period, and back to the streets and the bottle. When I had placed that call to Dorothy I had just emerged from County General Hospital, shaken and remorseful and as thirsty as ever.

Who can say what was going on in my mind when I dialed her number that night? Perhaps it was just a maudlin longing for something beautiful that had been lost in my past. Perhaps I needed another shoulder to cry on; my father's just wasn't big enough. It could have been either of these, but I prefer to think that I knew that from her I might find the peace I so desperately needed. Yet, even when she showed it to me I was unwilling to accept it.

All of this I told Dorothy, and more, that first night. When I had finished, weeping and barely able to choke out another word, she sat silently, looking at me with a solemn, intent expression. She waited a long moment before she spoke. When she did, it was from some deep reserve of certainty, some absolute knowledge of the truth beyond that moment.

"I know," she said, "that I love you. I guess I did from that very first day. Gary, whatever happens, whatever *had* happened, nothing can change that. The Lord has put us together, and it's something that can't be pulled apart by anything."

My sobbing slowed, and I raised my head to see the face that spoke these words. Something in the tone of her voice frightened me. That's the only word for it. It was as if you had waited all your life to hear something, and when it was finally spoken you discovered you didn't want to know it; that it required too much, that it said something about you that you couldn't face, that even the waiting was better than the knowing.

"I believe in you, Gary. I believe that my prayers will be answered. Maybe not tonight or tomorrow or a year from now, but they will be answered. You're too fine a man, too good to . . . finish this way."

"How do you know? How can you say that?" I asked, and a chill raced down my spine. Her eyes burned into mine as she answered me.

"I know. It's God's will."

CHAPTER TWENTY

Love Prevails

We were married six months later. It's a strange twist, I know, an almost unbelievable turnaround, a last chance at a time when all last chances should have exhausted themselves. What was this woman—this God-fearing, devout, clear-eyed mother and wife—doing by giving up a husband and a home (albeit not the happiest or most fruitful of marriages) to cast her lot with a time-tested loser? How could she have given it all up—a home, a steady income, a place in the community, and a future for her child—for something as dangerous and unknown as a future with me?

The answer, of course, is obvious. Even in the most adverse, most illogical, and most extreme conditions, love prevails. There was no doubt that Dorothy loved me and I loved her, but while I was completely incapable of demonstrating that love in any meaningful way, Dorothy, in faith and un- supported confidence, stepped into what by any measure seemed a doomed relationship. And it was not just she alone; she gave up *everything,* for herself *and* for Janet, to test the untried waters. She banked it all, as we might have said in Vegas, on a single, very long shot, and from the beginning it looked like the odds had beaten her.

I tried very hard at first to keep things tightly under rein. We rented an apartment in a quiet Los Angeles neighborhood, a palm-lined street filled with retired folks and lower-middle-class families. It seemed like the perfect setting for a new beginning, and I wanted to make the best of it.

I must have spent all of a week looking for gainful employment, holding off the drinking demon by consuming huge amounts of speed and pretending with my new bride that everything was on the up-and-up. Work, I'm sure, could have been found, but I was stubbornly unwilling to accept anything beneath my new "station"—that is, a man with a future, his past obliterated, a loving wife by his side, and all the old fallacies about high-blown destiny once again taking charge.

The speed, the Methedrine, and the amphetamines didn't help to sharpen my sense of reality. As anyone with experience with those vicious chemicals knows, the prevailing frame of mind resulting from prolonged use is paranoia supported by a raging case of megalomania. I wasn't getting the kind of employment I deserved because they were all out to get me, I reasoned (if reason is what you want to call it). They knew darned well that if they gave me chance I'd have *their* jobs in six months. They were keeping me down to save their own skins. With these and a dozen other fevered dillusions I allowed myself the luxury of "being too good for them."

As a result, Dorothy had to go to work to support us until I found "the right position."

Sitting at home day after day, watching TV and buzzing on speed like a bumblebee in a fruit jar, I naturally returned to short order to my old and dearest friend—alcohol. It's an interesting sidelight to my whole sordid tale up to this point that boredom often worked its insidious way with me, causing me to lapse into drunkenness simply as a way to pass the time. The bottle starts to look pretty good after half a day of soap operas, with the broad light of day streaming through the window and people on the street outside going about the business of living and working; you begin to feel a itch under your skin, the walls start closing in, and it's not so much a change of scenery that will do the trick as a change of consciousness. Obliterating any sense of time is the surest way to move those interminable afternoon hours along.

At first, I suppose, Dorothy accepted, even expected, my return to drinking. She had, after all, been warned, and it seemed she was as willing in those early days to deal with this monstrous side of me as she was willing to accept my desire to mend my ways for her sake. The first couple of times that she returned home from work to find me sprawled out on the living-room floor in a stupor, she was very matter-of-fact about getting me undressed and into bed, where I could sleep it off. Even those first few times that I would disappear for a day or two down to skid row to have a binge with my buddies (boozers the world around have the uncanny ability to form friendships in three seconds flat), she seemed to understand. There were no recriminations—no screaming fits and hurled rolling pins—and that, I think, bothered me more than if she *had* thrown a wifely tantrum.

This calm acquiescence to my increasingly loose hold on reality both puzzled and angered me. It was as if she didn't care enough to show concern, I thought to myself. Why couldn't I get a rise out of her? It is a measure of the degree to which my grasp on human relationships had slipped that the only way I was sure when I got through to someone was when he or she got angry or hurt, showed pity or disgust.

Dorothy demonstrated none of these, and it was only a matter of time before I tried to force the issue and bring to the surface those emotions I had so long depended on in others to show they still cared about poor old Gary Bell.

The cycles had set in with the regularity of the tides: sobriety with its attendant temptations and endless bouts with doldrums and self-recriminations, followed by eventual, inevitable surrender to the numbing embrace bought in bottles at the corner grocery store, followed by the rapid, now-comforting slide (as if I were returning home again). Then the nightmarish return to reality, with a head filled with cotton wadding, a mouth tasting like the bottom of a brewer's vat, and a gnawing in my stomach that felt like a swarm of malicious boll weevils. Drying out, sobriety, tearful vows, rigid adherence, stifling boredom, and the growing ache to escape—repeated time and time again that first year of our marriage.

One day as I awoke from a drunken stupor I heard a voice in the next room. "I don't know what to do," Dorothy was saying in a tone that was close to tears. The thought made me angry. Who was this person making my sweet Dorothy weep? "I can't go on without You. I need Your strength, Your power to overcome this." These were things she should be saying to me, I fumed, things she should be confiding in her husband. I heard the soft voices of others, whispering in agreement. To be saying this in front of others was just too much! It was . . . humilating! Then I heard my name spoken, and the sound of it on my wife's lips ripped through me like liquid fire.

"Gary is so helpless, so lost. Please Lord, look down on him in his condition and deliver him—" her voice was lost for a moment in a choking sob; "—deliver him from alcohol, Lord; bring him back to me, give him a new life, Lord. Give him a reason to live!"

She was praying! It was my turn then to choke back emotion—not sorrow or anguish or repentance, but blind, overwhelming rage. How dare she hold me up like some helpless child before this faceless god of hers and beg for help? How dare she embarrass me *and* herself by kowtowing and groveling on her knees before others, bringing up my problems for all to hear, hanging out our dirty laundry like a shameful flag? The room was swimming as my anger, abetted by the fact that I was still very drunk, washed over me. With a roar like a gored ox I charged into the living room.

There a half-dozen women kneeled with Dorothy on the carpet, their hands joined together, their faces upturned in various stages of shock and dismay at the horrifying sound issuing from my lips. With reddened and bulging eyes, dressed only in my underpants, I bellowed my disapproval in incomprehensible snorts and grunts. Anger turned to pain as my shin collided with the coffee table, sending cups and coffee flying and women scrambling to safety in the dining room. They watched with saucer eyes as I groveled around the floor amidst the growing brown stain leaking from the percolator. I was cutting my hands and knees on the broken china, and, lowing like some wounded animal, my hands made bloody imprints on the pages of the Bibles scattered all around me.

Finally I felt my wife's firm hands on my sweat-slicked shoulders, pulling me up and offering her body as support to guide me back to the bedroom. A cool towel on my forehead soothed and cleared my tormented thoughts as I passed fitfully from consciousness to a restless, vision-laden sleep. I don't know how long it was before I gained some sense of myself—the pains in my hands and knees, the stunned numbness of my brain, the burning shame in my heart—but there was a feeling of early morning, those quiet and still hours before dawn when I came to, opening my eyes and hearing Dorothy next to the bed, head bowed, hands folded, talking to a god I had never known . . . .

CHAPTER TWENTY-ONE

The Voice

The cycle grew tauter, the rut deeper, the circle of despair smaller and smaller. Dorothy and the love I had for her hardly mattered—she had become another way station on this terminal railway to hell. Her shelter was as good as, but certainly no better than, the garbage bins and flophouses I found myself increasingly drawn to. I *was* garbage, human debris—that was where I belonged.

This home, neat as a pin, filled at least with the hope and dreams of my daughter, if not Dorothy's or my own, became an affront to me. Why did it linger? Why didn't it fade away and leave me to the fate that had been carved out for me from the moment of my birth? It was a cruel charade, this reminder of what might have been—a lovely wife, a loving child, a place in the California sun. My home was in the shadows, among the ruins, stretched across the rubble of wasted potential and shattered illusions.

The fact that Dorothy clung so tenaciously—bringing me in off the streets when I crawled back sick and sore, cleaning me up and tending my wounds more times than can be counted, hoping, hoping, praying, and interceding, offering up again and again her own strength and faith in my place—that tireless, superhuman effort to salvage a man from the wreck of a life was no comfort to me. It was only a reminder of how far beyond the reach of love and care I really was. If Dorothy and the pure, unquenchable flame of her love could not light my way, then nothing on this earth could; if her arms could not drag me from the pit, then no one's could; if her breaking heart could not melt mine, then it was surely made of stone.

Skid row turned to hospitals, hospitals to sanatoriums, sanatoriums to mental institutions, and mental institutions back to skid row. It was one endless scene, an unrolling backdrop against which I played out the last desperate hours of my death wish. Doctors' faces, grim, stony, or shrugging off the inevitable, blended into one starched white visage; wards and private property rooms became a single huge, impersonal waiting room, where the seconds marked off the allotted space of suffering. Screaming drunks, perishing derelicts, shambling wrecks of humanity became the participants in this long wake, mumbling and nodding like a troupe of senile actors and actresses playing out their pathetic little roles in the sorrowful saga of Gary Bell. Pain was the master of the plot, a pain of life, of breath, of the heartbeat itself, that could not be numbed. Pain of 30-odd years in a hell of my creation, a pain of seeing reality trail away in wisps of fog. Pain so deep, so rooted, so agonizing that to destroy it would mean destroying the body that encased it, the mind that perceived it, the spirit that fed it. That became my reason for living: to find a way to die, and in death to find some lasting and unreachable peace, the peace of the yawning grave.

I was utterly incapable of effecting a single change, for better or worse, in my life. All that I have become since that time I owe to someone else. All that I have was given to me. All that I've done was done for me. And what is that, you might ask? What are Gary Bell's accomplishments? A reformed alcoholic, sober after all these years? Not trying to kill himself with quite the alacrity of his youth? Yes, all that and more. Success in worldly terms has been given me as well. I **am** the high-powered executive I always dreamed of being, making corporate decisons and big money deals. I **have** the nice car, the beautiful house, the respect and admiration of others, plus bonuses, vacations, travel, the good life. I enjoy a loving relationship with my wife and daughter. I'm able to provide for my aging father, participate in the community, tell a joke, enjoy a steak, feel the simple pleasure of a warm spring day. And did I earn all this? Did I pick myself by my own bootstraps, slap myself in the face, and say, ''Thanks, I needed that''?

I guess it would be nice for some people to answer yes to that question, to claim credit for turning themselves around and heading in the right direction. But it gives me a lot more pleasure to say no—I didn't do a lick of it. Sure, I worked hard to where I am in my business and social community, but everything I have, down to the shirt on my back and the paper in this typewriter, was a gift I didn't deserve—free and clear, a gift given to me for love.

It was not because I earned it, worked hard, or got all the breaks. What I have was given to me for love, and not because I had some great overpowering love that needed to be rewarded. No, all I had was the need; the love was there *for* me; the gift was offered without charge. I claimed my life because someone claimed it for me.

The cops picked me up in downtown L.A. in one seedy, grimy district overlooked by towering skyscrapers of chrome and steel. I'd been hanging out around a beer-and-wine bar for a week or so, running through some money I'd stolen from the house on my last furtive visit there and panhandling the price of a glass of sickening muscatel when that ran out. Finally, suffering from what felt like the onset of pneumonia, hacking and spitting up blood-flecked mucous, I had tried to make my way home, weaving in and out of the bustling downtown traffic, nearly getting run over more than once by the trucks barreling down Olympic Boulevard. I probably wasn't more than a couple of blocks from my temporary quarters, an alley behind the beer-and-wine joint, when the black-and-white police car pulled up and I was none-too-gently hustled into the back seat. With the weary sighs of too much experience, the cops drove me to the drunk tank at the county hospital.

I was a familiar face, a running joke really, but one whose punch line had long since gone stale. The doctor on duty recognized me immediately and told the officers it was no good leaving me there. In fact, they had been given instructions not to admit me to the county facilities on the chance that someone who could really be helped might not get treatment while I was taking up bed space. The doctor gave my escorts my home address—that is, the address where I came for money and a night's sleep—and told them to drop me there.

Drop me they did, right on the living-room floor. My stinking carcass lay at Dorothy's feet as she listened numbly to the cop's admonition that if I wasn't taken under supervision I was sure to get killed soon. It was an eventuality which they made very clear they weren't going to be responsible for; the implication, in fact, was that they were positively looking forward to it.

I don't know whether Dorothy wept or prayed for me that night. Perhaps by then her prayers and her tears had run dry. Her strength must have been flagging, for when I woke briefly the following morning I found myself again on the bed beneath the covers, yet this time my filthy rags were not neatly folded on the chair but were still clinging to me with layers of soot and sweat.

My first thought was, of course, for something to drink, but I found myself quite unable to move my legs. The fact was, I couldn't feel my body at all; consciousness had been reduced to a small knot of pain in my skull. It was with the greatest effort that I managed to pull from my tattered coat pocket a crumpled pack of cigarettes and with trembling fingers light one. Taking a few deep drags of the stale tobacco, I sighed deeply and passed again into unconsciousness.

A peculiar odor awoke me some time later—a pungent stench like burning wool or some smoldering animal fur. Shaking back the groggy shadows of my dreamless sleep, I opened my eyes to see a crowd of people in the bedroom—policemen, firemen in full regalia, the landlord, and in the middle Dorothy, dry-eyed but trembling. I heard Janet's voice, as if from very far away, calling to her mother, but I could not see my daughter. I wanted to call out to her and tell her that everything was all right, that there was nothing to worry about, but in truth I wasn't sure that was so. The room looked very strange to me, dark and ugly with black, greasy-looking marks marring the wallpaper and a tremendous stain, like a scorch from a hot iron, spread across the ceiling.

It was then that I remembered the cigarette I had started to smoke, and with it a hazy admonition from a fire-safety book of rules I couldn't recall reading, and the warning about smoking in bed, backed with scary statistics about death by such foolish oversight as this. But if everything else in the bedroom was charred or smoke-smudged, what was I doing alive? Or was I alive? In a sudden panic I jerked my head up and stared down the length of my body. I was there, all right, still wrapped in dirty rags, and all around me, in a rough oval shape, was a portion of unburnt mattress. What kind of miracle was this? I was thinking to myself as I heard a fireman talking to Dorothy.

"Your husband is a very lucky man, Mrs. Bell," he was saying. "If he hadn't urinated over the bed and himself, he'd certainly be a goner now."

So that was what had happened. I didn't know whether to laugh or cry, to hang my head in shame or crow over my good fortune. As it turned out, I didn't have much of a chance to do anything; wheels had already begun to turn.

Slowly, one by one, the official people filed out of the bedroom and the house, leaving only Dorothy and the landlord, an older man by the name of Mr. Feingold. Pretending to be asleep, I watched them from squinted eyes, straining to make out their whispered conversation.

"I'm sorry," Feingold said; "I know you can pay and the damages aren't even so much this time, thank God, but I can't take the risk, Mrs. Bell. The other tenants are complaining, and he comes in at all hours of the day and night. I've got to put a stop to this. You've got till the first of the month."

"But Mr. Feingold," Dorothy said, an edge of desperation to her voice, "what am I going to do? I'm working now, and I can't go out and look for another place to live. My daughter is in the middle of school, and I can't just take her out. She's been uprooted so much in the past few years. Couldn't you please—"

"I'm sorry, Mrs. Bell, I'd like to help, but—" he was interrupted by a sound coming from the bed, a strangled sob that, if it surprised him, utterly shocked me. I realized I was weeping large, uncontrolled tears, sobbing as I had not sobbed in years. I thought I had forgotten how to weep so freely, so flowingly, so innocently. It was as if I had returned in that moment to some childhood tragedy, a lost ball or a cruel word from a friend, and I wept with all the abandon of a small and helpless youngster in the throes of some very real upset. Only I was no child, and this was not a lost ball.

Silently Mr. Feingold took his leave, and Dorothy moved resolutely to the side of the bed, sitting down beside me and looking down on my tortured, shuddering body.

"I'm sorry, so very, very sorry, Dor—" the tears choked back the words and I longed for her to touch me, to lay a comforting hand on my brow, to stroke my cheek.

Her hands stayed in her lap, imprisoned by her determination to do, this time, the right thing for Janet and for herself.

"Gary," she began after a long and pregnant silence; "Gary, you know I love you very much. I always have and I always will. I want you to know that, darling, because we aren't going to be seeing each other for awhile.''

I struggled to rise, to protest, to look her in the eye and tell her it would never happen again. But it was no good—it wasn't true. What was to stop me from burning the whole house down the next time, with Janet and her and me in the flames? What was to stop me from having that next drink and the next one after that and after that? There wasn't a thing I could say to her; we both knew that.

"I'm going away with Janet, Gary," she continued, and although her voice was outwardly calm and composed I could hear the terrible tension lingering behind the words. "I can't live like this anymore. I've tried, Gary; I've prayed to the Lord for guidance, to tell me what is right, and I think He's shown me that this is what I must do. I've got to think of Janet, Gary. She needs at least one parent. There's nothing more I can do for you. I've reached the end of my resources. It's up to you now, Gary . . . you and God. But, darling, I want you to know that whenever you have come back . . to the man that you must have once been; whenever you stop drinking, Gary, I'll be there for you. I'm waiting, Gary, I'm waiting and praying." She too was crying now, her tears falling with mine to stain the ruined mattress. For a long time we wept together; it was the first act of togetherness we had shared in as long as I could remember. I held her hand, my face buried in her lap, smelling the cleanness of her clothes and the familiar scent of her perfume, drinking in these things that now seemed lost to me forever.

The doorbell rang. "That will be the hospital," Dorothy said gently, disengaging her hand from mine. "You'll be staying there for a week or so until you get on your feet." What would happen after that remained a question hanging in the air as she went to answer the door, admitting two attendants in starched white uniforms, carrying a stretcher.

It was in the ambulance, as the light of fading day shifted across the gleaming stainless steel and porcelain, that my life ended. With a tremendous yet soundless crash, my history fell in a heap around my ears, and for the first time in my long and miserable career I heard the voice of Gary Bell's salvation.

It was a voice, a very real voice speaking from somewhere deep inside my chest—a resonant, eternal sound that I can still hear clearly to this day.

Maybe you think I was a little off my rocker at this point. It's true that I had lost everything—a second family, a home, the only woman I had ever loved, maybe the only person who still loved or cared about me. Certainly I would be expected to become a little deranged, unhinged, call it what you will. I was still half-drunk, heading for one more in a series of clinical nightmares, with no prosspect of anything but more and ever more of the same. You're entitled to think that, I suppose, but I want you to be fairly warned before you decide I was having just another hallucination. I'm holding the trump card now, but before I lay it down, let me tell you what I heard.

It was time to stop, the voice told me. It was over now, and we—for that is what it called itself—we had reached the bottom. Now we would turn and go the other way. Now we would give it up—stop fighting, stop struggling, stop raging against our fate. The hour had come and the moment was at hand. We would turn ourself over now to a power that could accomplish what I had spent almost 30 years failing at. No more death, no more disease; our tears would be washed away. Trust, the voice said; trust, and we will be healed. Like a light breaking across a mountain chasm, I saw that the voice was right—I could be healed! The impossible could be done, and the time to start was now.

A sense of comfort such as I had never known swept over me, reaching deep down into the marrow of my bones to the burden I had for so long been bearing. A lifting, a lightness, brought with it a sense of giddiness the likes of which no drug could attain. It was the certainty more than anything else—the absolutely sure sense that this, at last, was right and good and true and real. I had found something, or rather something had found me, and in the finding I had been liberated from an existence doomed from the onset. I would survive, and more, I would flourish, because the voice had told me so. I had no power, no magic infusion of might. Trust, faith—that was what was required of me. That's all. No worlds of empty promises, no oceans of sorrowful might-have-beens—just belief that this force that had revealed itself to me could do what it promised. I would turn myself—body, mind and spirit—over to the voice and what the voice represented. I would turn myself over and die to struggle over and for all time. It was not my power, not my will, not even my life, but something or someone else's. It was an assurance that warmed me like the blessed sun after a torrential rain. Was it a crackpot's delusion? A fool's hope of a better life, another chance? The dream of a dying man? Maybe so; all I can state for sure are the facts: that day marked the last time alcohol ever passed my lips.

CHAPTER TWENTY-TWO

The First Step of Life

And so we come to the beginning of my story, for it was there, rocking back and forth in that ambulance, that my life began in earnest.

At first it was just an enabling. I say "just" because of the blessings which were to follow later. But at the time that enabling gave me the power to do what I had never done before and a meaning to life that I had never known before. These were gifts beyond compare. Suddenly I found myself with a will to do what was right, an insight into my need for alcohol and my flight from reality, a sense of the future and my place in it. It was as if I had been given the power to fly, to see the whole of my history and the vista of what was to come from an encompassing bird's-eye view. It was a feeling of liberation that one must feel after emerging from a long and famished wandering, lost in the wilderness but now coming onto a broad plateau and a straight and well-marked road.

What was it that I experienced in that eternal moment? What was it that made all the misery and pain that had come before simply a prelude to the real beginning of my life? That answer also was not denied to me. At first it was just the voice, an indwelling strength that I must have called on a hundred thousand times in the first months of my new existence. Every time my mind strayed to the comforts of the bottle, I could with miraculous results turn over my will again to the unknown power that dwelt within me.

I say miraculous because even as I sweated out those long moments when the temptation raged in my blood, I knew with certainty that I would prevail. Regardless of the urge, no matter what the twitches and spasms of my old nature, I could endure. Like the air I breathed, I became a fact of absolute reliance; this strength not my own was giving itself to me that I might live. There was an unshakable feeling in my gut that the power I had tapped into—or rather that had tapped into me, for I was, in that moment of revelation, as helpless to effect a single action as I had ever in my life been—that this power, by its very nature, could not fail, that there was simply nothing that could overcome what I now had dwelling inside me.

While the name and nature of my salvation were not kept from me, it was some time before I was given to know this identity. There was still much I had to learn, much I had to go through. How shall I describe that time, those first few years of my rebirth? It was marked, in the main, by the bestowal of gifts I had long thought were denied to me forever. Reconciliation was the first and foremost—with my father, with Dorothy, with my daughter Janet, and even to some degree with the ghosts of my past. Maybe it seems terrible that I could dismiss the pain and suffering I had caused so many for so long with a simple about-face, but I knew I had no choice if I were to live the life I had so longed about. I must let the dead bury the dead.

Before I knew forgiveness, like strength, was also available to me, I could say to myself, in those silent moments of crushing guilt, that the person who had committed those gross acts of injustice and cruelty was someone else. Does that sound like a cop-out? Maybe so, but I *felt* like a new person, and to carry the heavy baggage of my former life on my back like a deforming hump would have been to defeat every reason for which I had been rescued from that hell of my own making. In the eyes of men, in a court of law, I suppose I would be held accountable for these deeds, even if I could plead not guilty by reason of insanity.

But the voice inside told me a different story: the past is dead; Gary Bell is buried; look to the future; all else has been dealt with. I didn't know how; I couldn't quite figure out who was taking the rap for me, but I believed it. I could only look to the evidence of my own life to know that I was being told the truth, that hands more gentle than mine were drying tears of pain and hurt, that a heart more open than mine was accepting the burden of my victims as it had accepted me.

What would I say to those people whose lives I had so brutally intruded on if I were to meet them today? It's a fair question, and one I often asked myself. The answer is twofold: first I would ask for their forgiveness, and then I would share with them the forgiveness that had rescued me. It is all I can do, and more than enough, if they only understand one thing: the forgiveness I experienced is available to everyone, even them. If it's bitterness and hate they feel toward me, then I can't blame them, yet their bitterness and hate will be forgiven them as it was forgiven me.

Reconciliation, forgiveness . . . gifts beyond all reckoning. But there was more in store for me. Success was granted after so much failure. For the first time in my life I was given a chance to use **my** abilities and talents, to be rewarded in the world of business with accolades and real marks of achievement. But I learned something important on the way: it's all very nice to be an influential businessman, to wield power and make decisions; I mean that sincerely. It *is* nice, a good feeling, but only if you know what the *really* important things in life are—the real success story, the actual measure of happiness and security. I know it, and that's why being in the position I'm in today is as fulfilling as it is.

Reconciliation, forgiveness, success. What could be left for a man who has gone through what I have? Well, you're holding it in your hands. I have been given a chance to tell you my story, to lay it out for all to see, to put the tag end of triumph on the long trail of tragedy. You have suffered with me now as much as you were able. Maybe you had written me off back in prison, or in Vegas, or even before then, when I took that first fatal sip of the hard stuff. But I'm here, and I'm here not just to retrace the road of blood and guts behind me. That's a good story, I guess, full of suspense and cliff-hanging moments, but it's hardly enough. I've got more important things to say, and you've got more important things to hear.

I'm no preacher, no great religious thinker; what I know I learned the hard way, but I learned it. It took me years from that day in the ambulance to the night I realized the name of the power that had raised me from the dead, years to figure out that the person Dorothy and others kept telling me about was the same one who had the good work. It didn't take away from the lasting effect on my life, it didn't diminish the power or the glory that had entered in to claim me, it didn't make me any less a new man not to know the name of my Redeemer, but I'll tell you something—when I thanked Jesus Christ for saving Gary Bell, I knew for sure I was thanking the right Person.

CHAPTER
TWENTY-THREE

Tears of Thankful Joy

The air was sharp and the taste of a brisk approaching fall was on the breeze. The wide and comfortable streets of our neighborhood offered the casual path of our evening stroll. She held my hand and we moved in unison as one person, sharing sense and feeling with a single point of view.

What picture did we present that night to a casual observer, glancing out a living-room window at the couple walking arm-in-arm past their house? A long and happily married pair, prosperous and contented with their lot in life, fulfilled and satisfied with the simple joy of each other's company. Would any of that been evident from the way we looked at each other, the way we spoke, softly yet with a sense of urgency? Could we have provided some clue as to what had come before and what was to follow? Was there a way to know that from such a simple act, a stroll along a darkened suburban byway, the quest of a lifetime would reach its joyous conclusion?

It was early in what by all estimations must be considered my meteoric rise up the executive ladder, a rise marked with its fair share of ambition and infighting. While I still depended for balance on the inner voice which had spoken to me almost three years before, it still gave me a deep sense of satisfaction to finally achieve the goals I had set for myself as a young man: success in the world of business, respect and standing. These were things to which I attached great importance.

If it seems, in retrospect, that perhaps I sought *too* avidly the accolades of success and its financial rewards, I offer this single justification: I didn't yet know who I really served. Certainly I had stopped in my busy upward climb to reflect on the heights and depths of my life; certainly I looked back more than a few times, back and down to what I had emerged from. And as I looked, the nameless face looked back, the voice whose power had rescued me from hell. Nothing of my good fortune had anything to do with my will or resolve. Something else, some*body* had taken mercy on me. Standing now in the full light of day, a bright day where the future looked certain and sure, I knew that if it hadn't been for this stranger, I would have been just another statistic.

For me, the experience in the ambulance was personal: it answered to my needs so directly that I couldn't imagine that it was in any way a shared experience. There was no religious jargon, no simple catch-phrase or set of preconceptions, that explained what had happened to me. "Saved," "redeemed"—those are just words. What can be said to describe the giving of breath to the body of a corpse, the blind eyes suddenly seeing, death swallowed up in victory? Nothing anybody told me made any sense of it, and yet the nameless presence had stayed with me since that day.

Even as Dorothy and I made our way through the soft and peaceful night, her words were incomprehensible. It was only her tone, the love and peace that warmed it, which kept me listening in such rapt attention. I guess it was on that night that I understood more about Dorothy than I had known since I first met her, a lifetime ago in Tucson—that calm center, the unshakable reserve of strength and peace, the gentle yet frank look of her eyes. What was hidden there? I had asked myself a thousand times.

"It was Jesus Christ who brought you back," Dorothy said, "to me."

The sound of traffic on the freeway, off to the foot of the hills, whispered in the night, and I heard myself saying, "I've heard that a thousand times."

"It was true every time."

We passed beneath a street light and she stopped. Turning to face me, my wife smiled, but her eyes looked straight and unwaveringly into mine.

"Gary," she said, "do you ever think about all those years . . . before?"

"Of course."

"And do you ever think of what might happen if you had it all to do over again?"

I had to be honest. "I don't think I'd live through it." I replied with a rueful smile, and was grateful when she answered me with a sudden embrace.

"I want you to know," she said as I smelled the fragrance of her hair, "I want you to understand how you were chosen . . . by God . . . for something special."

"This moment."

"Yes, this moment and others. But more; Gary, can't you see that you were being held apart? You've come through all this for a purpose."

I wasn't listening just then. My mind took me back . . . to all the bottles and pills and sick screaming mornings. I remembered the handfuls of speed I washed down with straight vodka, the dozens of alcoholic convulsions, any one of which could have snapped my mind for good. And more: the terrified face of the woman lying on the floor as a masked man pulled a trigger and a loud click filled the air. I could live with a lot of things; could I have lived with murder? They rose then, the faces of my victims, and I knew suddenly what Dorothy meant about being "held apart." Not only had I been kept alive, safe at last from hurling myself into the black abyss, but somehow all of what had happened to me in my poor, sad existence had been dealt with. That was the only way I could explain it, the only phrase I could attach to this unshakable feeling that I didn't have to live with the ghosts of my past. They had been removed somehow, separated from me, and, as a leading authority has it, were as far away from me as the East is from the West.

I did not realize that Scripture promises this very thing. I had never read the Bible, but had only listened with closed ears to people tell me about "redemption" and "salvation," using them as words in a language I couldn't understand. But when Dorothy spoke again, a feeling of dumbstruck awe overwhelmed me.

"Look at yourself, Gary; look what He's doing for you. He's given you a reason to live. He's forgiven you." Her voice resonated with passion and conviction, her words penetrating some secret core of truth that began to flutter and stir.

There was a long pause. Forgiven . . . the word rang like a bell. Forgiven. But how? I must have asked the question out loud, for Dorothy answered immediately.

"Look beyond the words, Gary. *Hear* what I'm saying. It's truth, living truth. Imagine what it would be like without it, if you had to *answer* for it all."

I shuddered, her words too harsh, the implications too frightening.

"Forgiven," the word escaped my thoughts and became a mutter as I tried to circle the urgent message hovering behind Dorothy's words.

"There's a lot to answer for, darling, but we don't have to worry. It's been taken care of." It was as if she saw into the window of my soul, speaking the truths I felt there. "Acknowledge what you already know," she said, her words a soft, insistent pushing against this quavering sense of expectation that was overtaking me.

A wash of calm, a perception of beauty such as I had never known, a promise of peace—how could I hear so much of these in Dorothy's simple words?

"You know Him, Gary. You told me so yourself. You seek Him every day. And He's here." I knew then, without looking, that tears were glistening in her eyes, and I felt the rush of my own tears flooding my vision after what seemed a wait of a million years.

It was the sound of her prayer, a voice transfixed with a kind of love that I had never known, a fervent thanksgiving issuing from some deep well of reverence and gratitude, that brought to me the astonishing revelation that God loved me.

"Thank You, Lord," she prayed; "thank You for revealing Yourself to Gary. Thank You for saving his life. Praise You, Lord, thank You." It was the faith, the absolute confidence she had, that gave her words an electric power. She was claiming me in the name of the One who had claimed us all, who had claimed me for life, the One who had brought me to this moment when His name became for me an answer to a lifelong prayer, a prayer whose words I didn't know, but whose plea I felt like a sharp ache.

I looked at my wife; I watched as the wind ruffled her hair and the light of the lamp above us sparkled in her eyes. Together we wept, and in weeping we gave thanks.

CHAPTER TWENTY-FOUR

This Is The Lord I Serve

"Flight 703 to Seattle is now departing from Gate 52."

"Mr. Collins, white courtesy telephone, please"

"The red zone is for immediate loading and unloading of passengers only."

Around me, families hurried by, arms full of suitcases and squalling children. Couples embraced, oblivious to the chaos around them, and harried businessmen shot frightened glances at their watches as they rushed to keep a schedule.

Inside the phone booth a sense of unbearable expectation kept the sights and sounds of the busy Dallas Airport a world away. All I could hear, all I knew, was the ring of the phone hundreds of miles away, and the breathless suspense that kept me hanging onto the reciever. I was torn in that moment between dropping the phone, flying out of that booth, and getting as far away as possible, and the equally strong sense of joy, of something long undone but now at last completed. This was a moment for which I had waited over ten years, and like any life-turning event, I faced it with a mixture of happiness and dread.

Someone picked up the phone. It was a voice I didn't recognize. How could I? The last time I had heard it was when its owner was barely four years old.

"Hello," the voice was firm and strong, yet I could hear clearly the pitch of intense excitement.

"Jerri?" There was no way to keep the tremor out of my voice.

"Daddy."

Maybe all those people, rushing to and fro to some distant destination, would have wondered at the sight of a grown man weeping unashamedly in an airport telephone booth. Perhaps some of them even stopped, wondering if there was something they should do to help. If they were there, I couldn't see them. I was blind with the simple joy of hearing those two syllables spoken.

It wasn't for years after becoming a Christian, learning to trust that inner voice that told me what God's will was for my life, that I finally was able to work up the courage to delve into a dark and embittered past. I guess if it had been up to me, I would have simply let things alone. Every cliche about burying the past, crying over spilt milk, and water under bridges must have come up thousands of times after my new life began. After all, I had been given a fresh beginning: I had a beautiful wife and two loving children; I was one of the top executives in my field and had recently started my own company, Canon Recruiting Systems; drugs, alcohol, and the specter of death were all things of the past; I could look forward to a life filled with the spirit of love, from my family and the Lord.

What was missing? Why did my thoughts return over and over again to the image of Jerri sitting and crying in her crib, playing on my lap, or simply staring up at me with deep, trusting eyes? Surely she was better off now, better freed from the pain and recrimination of the past. Whatever she had known of me, whatever she remembered or was told, was enough for her now. Let her live her own life . . ..

It didn't work. I couldn't shake the conviction that I had to contact my first daughter, if only to know that she was alive and doing as well as a fatherless child could be expected to do. Finally, after months of soul-searching and prayer, I contacted a private detective and gave him the last address I had for Darlene and Jerri.

I remember thinking that the man did his work a little *too* well, for scarely a month later he returned with the whereabouts of my first family. The information he provided was not much more heartening. Darlene was remarried and now lived in a prosperous section of Phoenix with her second husband and Jerri. From all outward signs they needed me intruding into their life like they needed a second head. Yet something had been set in motion, something frightening and yet at the same time so close to me that it could not be denied. I had to carry through with my intent. Dorothy and the kids, for their part, were supportive and encouraging. I think they knew what I was going through, and how much seeing Jerri again really meant to me.

Jerri was, in many ways, my only link to a past that I had all but thrown away; she was the only memory of any happiness I had during the whole interminable misery of my early adulthood. Could

I just toss that away? Could I pretend that what I had felt for her was gone, had never existed? I knew the answers to those questions even as I sat down to draft a letter to her, the hardest letter I have ever composed. I can say now that without the help of the Holy Spirit I would never been able to put down a single line, much less a full page.

"How does one contact someone they love very much, but have purposely stayed out of their life for over 13 years?" the letter began. The answer, like the answer to those other questions, was a simple one, but a hard one. I had no choice. The Lord had put it in my heart to complete the cycle I had begun that lifetime ago, to find the love I had lost and to make a beginning in healing the wounds.

"I am hoping that you don't have any animosity toward me," the letter concluded, "However, if you do I can appreciate it. While living with you and your mother, I was a miserable person. Your mother made a very intelligent decision to get you and herself out of that situation. I offer no excuses for my past behavior—just a sincere apology for the pain, hurts, and hardships that I caused you or your mother.

"Believe me, I don't want to ignite any old hurts or try to come between you and your parents. My only motivation in contacting you is to establish a line of communication or to meet one another in person and reacquaint ourselves with each other. Again, it's your decision. I sincerely hope and pray that your decision is in the affirmative."

I'm not sure I knew what was going to happen when I was paged at the airport, on my way from Dallas (where I was concluding a business deal) back to Los Angeles. It was Dorothy on the line, and when she told me that Jerri had called and wanted to speak to me something leaped in my heart like a rambunctious kid, while at the same time I felt like sinking into the floor. Well, I thought to myself after hanging up, there's nothing to do now but to see it through. And I placed the fateful call.

I didn't go back to Los Angeles that night. Instead I took a direct flight to Phoenix to meet Darlene and Jerri for dinner. Darlene looked well and happy, but there was a terrible nervousness between us. I knew that so much had happened, so many deep wounds, and that our lives were so far apart now, that it was useless to try to bridge the gap. Perhaps that strikes you as a lack of faith, for it's true that the Lord can heal any wound. All I offer in evidence is what Darlene later told Jerri about that meeting. That, she said to our daughter, was the man I had married, the man I saw behind the drunken cruelty. For her, as well as for myself, the thought of what could have been simply too painful to endure, and why, after all, should it be endured? The sins of the past had been forgiven, God had blessed each of us in his bountiful grace, tears had been wiped away, and each of us could look life squarely in the face. Was that not enough for anyone?

Yet what existed between Jerri and me was another matter. Beginning at that first dinner and continuing through her subsequent visits to my new family, and deepening in the many heart-to-heart talks which we have shared since our reuniting, Jerri and I have reaffirmed a bond that is strong and unwavering. Knowing her again, being able to see that she has grown into a wise and compassionate young woman, has perhaps been the greatest blessing of my new life.

It is as if God, having provided everything that He did to bring me up from the depths and make me anew, crowned His new creature with joy and contentment beyond measure. God's love is infinite, and in it I found not only myself but my past.

It would have been enough, I suppose, to see, talk, and hold Jerri again. It would have been enough to know that the past was forgiven. It would have been enough to offer to her what I could from my life and experiences. But the Lord doesn't stop at enough. On that very first night, standing outside her Phoenix home, looking into the blazing clear night flung wide with stars, I told her about the love God had poured out upon me.

"I know, Daddy," she said softly; "I know the love of Jesus too."

This is the Lord I serve.

For further information:

Mr. Gary W. Bell, President
Canon Management Corporation
One Wilshire Building Suite 1210
One Wilshire Boulevard
Los Angeles, California 90017